The News Media

Other books in the Careers for the Twenty-First Century series:

Aeronautics

Law Enforcement

Medicine

Careers for the Twenty-First Century

The News Media

By Peggy J. Parks

LUCENT BOOKS
SAN DIEGO, CALIFORNIA

THOMSON
GALE

*Detroit • New York • San Diego • San Francisco
Boston • New Haven, Conn. • Waterville, Maine
London • Munich*

Library of Congress Cataloging-in-Publication Data

Parks, Peggy J., 1951–
The news media / by Peggy J. Parks.
p. cm. — (Careers for the 21st century)
Summary: Covers the various positions available in the field of print and broadcast journalism, discussing qualifications, training, job opportunities, and technological advances.
Includes bibliographical references and index.
ISBN 1-59018-205-7 (alk. paper)
1. Journalism—Vocational guidance—Juvenile literature. [1. Journalism—Vocational guidance. 2. Vocational guidance.] I. Title. II. Careers for the 21st century (San Diego, Calif.)
PN4797 .P337 2002
070.4'023—dc21

2001007987

Printed in the U.S.A.

Contents

Foreword

Young people in the twenty-first century are faced with a dizzying array of possibilities for careers as they become adults. However, the advances of technology and a world economy in which events in one nation increasingly affect events in other nations have made the job market extremely competitive. Young people entering the job market today must possess a combination of technological knowledge and an understanding of the cultural and socioeconomic factors that affect the working world. Don Tapscott, internationally known author and consultant on the effects of technology in business, government, and society, supports this idea, saying, "Yes, this country needs more technology graduates, as they fuel the digital economy. But . . . we have an equally strong need for those with a broader [humanities] background who can work in tandem with technical specialists, helping create and manage the [workplace] environment." To succeed in this job market young people today must enter it with a certain amount of specialized knowledge, preparation, and practical experience. In addition, they must possess the drive to update their job skills continually to match rapidly occurring technological, economic, and social changes.

Young people entering the twenty-first-century job market must carefully research and plan the education and training they will need to work in their chosen career. High school graduates can no longer go straight into a job where they can hope to advance to positions of higher pay, better working conditions, and increased responsibility without first entering a training program, trade school, or college. For example, aircraft mechanics must attend schools that offer Federal Aviation Administration–accredited programs. These programs offer a broad-based curriculum that requires students to demonstrate an understanding of the basic principles of flight, aircraft function, and electronics. Students must also master computer technology used for diagnosing problems and show that they can apply what they learn toward routine maintenance and any number of needed repairs. With further education, an aircraft mechanic can gain increasingly specialized licenses that place him or her in the job market for positions of higher pay and greater responsibility.

In addition to technology skills, young people must understand how to communicate and work effectively with colleagues or clients from diverse backgrounds. James Billington, librarian of Congress, ascertains that "we do not have a global village, but rather a globe on which there are a whole lot of new villages . . . each trying to get its own place in the world, and anybody who's going to deal with this world is going to have to relate better to more of it." For example, flight attendants are increasingly being expected to know one or more foreign languages in order for them to better serve the needs of international passengers. Electrical engineers collaborating with a sister company in Russia on a project must be aware of cultural differences that could affect communication between the project members and, ultimately, the success of the project.

The Lucent Books Careers for the Twenty-First Century series discusses how these ideas come into play in such competitive career fields as aeronautics, biotechnology, computer technology, engineering, education, law enforcement, and medicine. Each title in the series discusses from five to seven different careers available in the respective field. The series provides a comprehensive view of what it's like to work in a particular job and what it takes to succeed in it. Each chapter encompasses a career's most recent trends in education and training, job responsibilities, the work environment and conditions, special challenges, earnings, and opportunities for advancement. Primary and secondary source quotes enliven the text. Sidebars expand on issues related to each career, including topics such as gender issues in the workplace, personal stories that demonstrate exceptional on the job experiences, and the latest technology and its potential for use in a particular career. Every volume includes an Organizations to Contact list as well as annotated bibliographies. Books in this series provide readers with pertinent information for deciding on a career, and a launching point for further research.

Introduction

Keeping the Public Informed

When an event occurs halfway across the globe or in their hometown, people depend on news media professionals to bring them news about the event. Whether written in a newspaper story or broadcast on the television or radio, the news keeps people informed about what is going on in the world. And they have a right to be kept informed—the First Amendment to the U.S. Constitution guarantees freedom of speech and freedom of the press, which forms the fundamental principle embraced by the news media: the people's right to know.

There are many different kinds of topics that constitute news. A feature story might focus on a foreign country and its people and culture, or on a local environmental issue. A "hard news" story might focus on a major fire, airplane crash, bomb scare, or robbery. A political story might focus on an upcoming election and the candidates who are running for office. Television photojournalist Carl Filoreto discusses how radically news topics can vary:

> We've covered hurricanes, train wrecks, myriad automobile accidents, fires of all kinds, police shootings, gang riots, Ku Klux Klan rallies, floods, bank robberies, avalanches, and countless homicides . . . a big part of the job is gritting your teeth and doing your job as well as you can while you cover things that are grim, tragic, or distasteful . . . [but] we also handle plenty of upbeat features, boring city council meetings, and community notables.[1]

There are different ways of communicating news to the public. Newspapers provide it in printed form, and television and radio stations broadcast the news. Each of these divisions of the media receives news leads in a variety of ways. Most national and international news comes into the newsroom from the wire services, which are news-gathering organizations like the Associated Press and United Press International that transmit via satellite. Most local news comes from a combination of sources and activities. "Tipsters," or people who call newsroom assignment desks or news hotlines to report things they observe, are an important source of local information as are the courts and police and fire departments. Media staff, including reporters, writers, and non-news employees, also provide news leads.

People are often intrigued by the professionals who work in the news media. Some are more visible than others, but all play a vital role in keeping the public informed. Reporters seek out newsworthy information and report it, both in print and in the broadcast media. Photojournalists travel to sites where news is happening and create stories through their cameras. Television newscasters, or anchors as they are commonly known, are the most visible news media professionals, as they read the news on television. Broadcast producers are behind-the-scenes professionals who are crucial to the success of television and radio programming. Radio announcers sometimes fulfill the double role of on-air personality and newscaster.

Because news media professionals are the first to find out about news and are frequently in the center of the action, they are often perceived as leading lives that are exciting, glamorous, and sometimes dangerous. In the case of a major television news anchor or reporter covering world events, this could certainly be an apt description, but it probably would not apply to a columnist at a small-town newspaper or a radio announcer at a small station. Still, while news media careers can differ widely, everyone in this field has one thing in common: a responsibility to keep the public informed.

Another commonality among news media professionals is that they know better than to expect the usual nine-to-five routine of some other careers. There is no such thing as a typical day. Everything that happens is dictated by that day's breaking events, and everything varies based on what needs to be done in order to get the news out. Schedules can be erratic, with long hours and tight

Television anchor Peter Jennings speaks during a news broadcast. News media professionals keep the public informed of world events.

deadlines. For some in the news media, long-distance travel is necessary at the last minute. And there is always tremendous pressure to get the news in front of the people as fast as possible.

News media careers are popular and highly sought after, so competition among newcomers is tough. Students in middle school and high school who are interested in a news media career should do everything possible to expose themselves to the news, both by reading a newspaper every day and by watching the news on television. Hands-on experience is also important: Writing for school newspapers and yearbooks is an excellent way to get started, as is volunteering after school and on weekends at a local newspaper, radio station, or television station. With most careers in the news media, a four-year college degree is a must.

In spite of the fierce competition and the unpredictability of the work most people with careers in the news media could not imagine doing anything else. They share a natural curiosity as well as a tendency to work better when they are challenged. Reporter Seth Mydans, Southeast Asia correspondent for *The New York Times*, describes the passion that is typical of a news professional:

> Do you want to know what an exploding volcano looks like, or a World Series game, or a new virus under a microscope, or the latest fashions, or a tent city filled with refugees? Do you want to sit down and talk with a governor or a serial killer or a ballerina? And if you are moved by what you witness, don't you want to try to communicate what you saw and felt? The great thing about being a journalist is that you aren't just a tourist; what you experience is raw material for trying to write in the most compelling way. You're the eyes and ears of all the people who couldn't stand there beside you to watch the volcano explode.[2]

Chapter 1

Reporters

Reporters are responsible for keeping the public informed about news. It is their job to seek out and gather information that people need and want to know and to turn it into stories that are printed in newspapers or broadcast on the television or radio. Reporters play an important role in our society because their stories inform the public about things that are happening in the local community, the state, the nation, and the world.

People choose to become reporters for a variety of reasons, but they generally have one thing in common that leads them into a news career: a natural, somewhat insatiable curiosity that is sometimes referred to as a "nose for news." Seth Mydans from *The New York Times* shares his perspective on being a reporter: "I've always been curious about things, and journalism is the best field to indulge your curiosity. It gives you an excuse to sneak into places where you're not supposed to be, to ask direct questions and learn intimate things about powerful or interesting people and to be in the front rows, or front lines, as history is being made."[3]

How Reporters Find and Report News

Although reporters may work in different types of media—television, radio, or newspapers—they all have similar responsibilities. And no matter where they work, a reporter's number-one task is to track down the news and report it.

When they receive leads and news tips, reporters must quickly investigate them to determine if the information is based on fact or rumor. When they learn about something newsworthy, they are "on the scene" to interview victims, witnesses, and/or officials. Reporters take notes, either by hand or using tape recorders or laptop computers. Following their interviews they may need to dig up additional facts by talking with other individuals or by doing background research.

After gathering the material they need, newspaper reporters usually return to their offices to organize their information, determine the "angle" (main point) of their stories, and then write the articles. If they have been given a special assignment in a remote location such as another state or a different part of the world, they can send their stories to the newspaper via e-mail. If reporters are extremely busy covering multiple stories at once or trying to meet tight deadlines, their editors or producers may assign staff writers to write the stories for them.

Unlike newspaper reporters, broadcast reporters (who work in radio and television) sometimes compose stories and report them live from wherever the news is happening. When they report live from the scene, broadcast reporters must think fast and prepare their

Broadcast reporters conduct a live interview. A reporter's number-one task is to find the news and report it.

work rapidly, even while the story is happening around them. Journalism professor Vernon Stone tells how reporters typically feel about reporting the news live on the air: "It's often exciting. You're in the middle of what's happening. What you do in your job can make a difference in the world. It's satisfying to know you're communicating information that many people need or want to know. And that you've done a good job of it. If you're on the air, your face or voice may be familiar, which may hold appeal for you."[4]

When broadcast reporters cover stories that are taped for a later news program, they gather the information and return to the studio to review and edit their tapes. They may add additional background facts or details and then finalize their story before it is put on the air. These taped stories usually take a long time to prepare—a story that is on the air for only sixty seconds could take as long as ten hours to research and develop, based on how complicated and involved it is.

Sometimes reporters receive leads that require complicated investigations and lengthy research. In this case an "investigative reporter," sort of a Sherlock Holmes of the media, may spend days, weeks, or even months meticulously following up on leads and gathering information. The resulting story could reveal any number of things, either positive or negative. It might increase awareness of and support for a previously unknown organization. It might identify the need for changes in existing laws and regulations or expose a criminal or a group of criminals. Investigative reporters perform an important function: The awareness that is generated as a result of their stories can motivate the public to react in response and help implement change.

Qualities Reporters Need

In order to be successful all reporters must be naturally inquisitive and interested in everyone and everything making news. They must be aggressive and persistent in tracking down story leads and facts, but they must balance that with compassion and genuinely care about people. Author Ted White, formerly with CBS News in New York, writes about the passion reporters share:

> Reporters must be concerned, sometimes alarmed, often angered and always caring about the major problems that face the community and world in which we live. Reporters often can do little to correct injustice or unfairness, or the

Reporters, such as those seen here, must be aggressive and persistent when tracking a news story.

misery, suffering, and critical problems of certain segments or groups in our society, but they should have a desire to do so. Their weapons are enlightenment and information.[5]

Reporters constantly interact with all kinds of people including witnesses, victims and their families, police and other emergency workers, and even curious onlookers. This means they must be poised, confident, and have excellent listening and communication skills. They must also remain cool and calm in the face of any kind of crisis about which they might be reporting. When interviewing people who are victims of crime or who have been involved in tragedies, it is important for reporters to exercise good manners and tact in their interview techniques and not be overly aggressive. As NBC news correspondent Bob Dotson explains, "You never go up to someone who has great grief and act like a stereotypical journalist or you are going to go out on your ear, or worse."[6]

The term "responsible journalism" means reporting the facts and only the facts, so it is essential for reporters to be committed to providing accurate and impartial information. They must report without

A reporter interviews a candidate at a political rally.

prejudice despite their own personal views on a subject or event. For instance, if a reporter has a personal dislike for a particular political candidate, he or she must put those feelings aside when interviewing the candidate for a story. And no matter what the nature of the news is—from reporting the grand opening of a mall to a major fire or serious accident, from a political rally to an oil spill in the local river—reporters must make sure the information reported is factual and not based on rumor or speculation. There is a phrase that is familiar to everyone in the news media: "Getting it fast is no good unless it's right" and reporters must always keep that in mind. Keith Bradsher, Detroit bureau chief for *The New York Times*, talks about a reporter's responsibility to seek out the truth and only report facts: "When news happens, it is my job to find out the details as quickly as possible and with complete accuracy. One of the hardest parts of the job is figuring out where the truth lies. Many people present only some of the facts and choose the ones that favor their position. A good reporter talks to as many people as possible so as to learn as much as possible about the subject."[7]

Because they need to track down so much information, reporters need excellent research skills, with a good understanding of how to find what they need. For instance, when covering a story they may need additional or supporting information about the topic from the

Internet, the public library, or their own newsroom "morgues," which hold the back issues of magazines, newspapers, and tapes of video or audio news stories from the past. Reporters also must have good writing skills to clearly present their facts and thoughts into stories that interest the public. And because they are perpetually faced with looming deadlines and disruptions, reporters must be disciplined and organized, yet flexible and able to cope with change.

Market Size and Rankings

In terms of broadcasting, "market" simply refers to a geographical area. The United States has over two hundred television markets and nearly three hundred radio markets, each of which includes a city and surrounding areas that are served by a group of television or radio stations. Large markets include New York, Chicago, Los Angeles, Atlanta, and Miami, as well as other major cities. In general, the larger the market, the greater the number of television and radio stations located in that market.

A market's numerical size, or "ranking" (not to be confused with "rating"), is determined by the number of homes with television sets or radios located in that market. Two markets may be essentially identical in physical size, but the one with the largest population—and thus the largest number of potential viewers or listeners—will be ranked larger. For example, Salt Lake City, Utah, is physically larger than New York City. However, in market rankings New York is number one while Salt Lake City is number thirty-six. This is because even though Salt Lake City is larger, its population (including surrounding areas) is approximately 1 million people, while New York City's population (including surrounding areas) is nearly 20 million people.

Market size can influence a number of factors. For example, advertisers pay for commercials according to the potential size of the audience, so the amount of money a radio or television station spends on its various departments, including news, usually depends on market size. In addition, market size determines the number of people employed by radio and television stations as well as the money they make; those in larger markets almost always earn significantly higher salaries than those in smaller markets.

Working Conditions

Flexibility is especially important because reporters are often on the go much of the time. In fact, reporters sometimes joke that their offices are actually in their cars. Their days often are spent traveling around as they follow up story leads, conduct interviews, and verify information. While some of their time is spent in the newsroom, as soon as a lead comes in they are off again visiting crime scenes, reporting on accidents, and tracking down any other information they might need.

The newsroom of a television or radio station or newspaper is almost always crowded and noisy. These places are filled with the sounds of computers, printers, fax machines, pagers, police and fire scanners, and telephones, as well as an ongoing chorus of people's voices as they obtain information on the phone or talk to each other about leads. Joe Grimm of the *Detroit Free Press* describes a typical newspaper newsroom: "You'll find it is one of the busiest, writingest, artsiest, computingest, talking-on-the-telephoningest, finding-outingest places you've ever seen. One reason is, today's newspaper is as fresh as today. It has to be. Look at one. It even has today's date on it. That means that newspaper people are busy people. Very."[8]

Along with a chaotic work environment, reporters must also deal with constant unpredictability in their jobs. *New York Times* reporter Tamar Lewin describes how this uncertainty is actually part of the appeal for people in her line of work:

> One of the best parts of being a reporter is that all your days are different, and you never quite know what's going to happen next. So I might come in to the office, expecting to spend the day doing interviews and research for a long story on grandparents' rights, and discover, instead, that there's been a big plane crash or an important court decision, and that I have to leap in to write a quick story for that afternoon. There's just no routine. . . . Some days I'm on the phone all day, asking questions and gathering information. Some days I stay home and write. Other days I'm running downtown to talk to a women's rights group or flying off to look at a preschool in Texas.[9]

This unpredictability is the same in all branches of the media. Filoreto says there is no such thing as a "typical" day in a television newsroom because even though a day might start off slowly, things can change at any time. He explains: "No matter what job you hold in the newsroom, you must always be ready to change gears. What starts as a predictable, unexciting news day can end as a day you'll always remember."[10]

The Downside of Being a Reporter

In addition to constantly expecting the unexpected, savvy reporters are well aware that they have not chosen a quiet, sedate career. In fact, it is quite the opposite. All reporters must learn to work in spite of distractions and be able to tune them out as they concentrate on compiling information and writing their stories. These distractions, coupled with seemingly impossible deadlines, can provide stress-filled days and schedules that often include nights, weekends, and holidays.

While a reporter's job can be exciting, it also carries a certain amount of risk and is sometimes dangerous. Wherever the news is—in a faraway war-torn country or a remote region in the United States—reporters are there to cover the story in the midst of the danger and chaos. Filoreto describes some of the situations reporters face and how they must handle them:

A reporter is attacked while covering a story in Israel's West Bank. Some reporters work in dangerous settings.

> Good reporters must be willing to get their hands dirty. . . . They've got to be willing to be blown around by a hurricane, to walk through the city landfill, to don a gas mask during combat, and to do a live report on traffic conditions on a dismal overpass above a nondescript highway during a snowstorm. In short, they've got to be prepared to go where the news is, no matter what the conditions, and then make some sense of it once they get there.[11]

During dangerous situations it can be difficult for reporters to report only factual, unbiased news. Elizabeth Pisani, a correspondent for *Asia Times*, explains:

> In a climate of fear, you are more likely to believe what you are told and less likely to investigate what you are told. The danger to work quality is very real for every journalist in a difficult situation. Sources are more difficult to check out, information is more difficult to confirm and the general navigation required to complete a story thoroughly is jeopardised if the journalist is working in fear, whether the reporter is working on a story about a rebel group or a Mafia crime ring.[12]

The result of working under these types of conditions can be self-censorship by the reporter, which leads to a story being biased and not completely factual. Therefore, while reporters cannot always control the stories to which they are assigned nor the situations around them, they can prepare themselves by being aware of the dangers involved and communicating with their editors or producers when those dangers could influence their stories.

Becoming a Reporter

Even with the risks and unpredictability involved in a news media career, many people want to be reporters, so the field is extremely competitive. It takes years of hard work, determination, and perseverance to become a reporter and to achieve success. Therefore, it is important to start preparing early—even as early as middle school or high school.

Courses such as English, history, government, and geography provide a good foundation for an aspiring reporter, as do foreign language courses, speech, journalism, and communications. And as

Reporters cover a story about a sniper during the war in Bosnia. Successful reporters must be prepared to go where the news is, even in times of danger.

with many careers today, a college degree is essential. Reporters almost always have bachelor's degrees in journalism, English, or other liberal arts fields, and some have master's degrees. They must have a keen understanding of the world around them as well as a broad knowledge of history, business, science, the arts, politics, geography, and foreign affairs.

Aspiring reporters should also seek out as much hands-on experience as possible, as *New York Times* reporter Keith Bradsher confirms:

> The best way to become a reporter is to start writing for a high school newspaper. If your school does not have a newspaper, ask a teacher if it might be possible to start one. You could write articles about the school and post them on your Web site. I learned on my high school newspaper that I loved to write articles and have kept writing them ever since, first on my college paper and then professionally. Reading newspapers regularly is valuable. It teaches you how to present information in a clear, succinct fashion. And it gives you a broad perspective on everything from foreign policy to finance and science.[13]

The Power of Investigative Reporting

On a Saturday in 1972, a young *Washington Post* reporter was called into the newspaper's office and given an assignment. The Democratic National Committee headquarters, located in the Watergate Hotel in Washington, D.C., had been burglarized and the reporter, Bob Woodward, was to work with fellow reporter Carl Bernstein in covering the story. What followed was an investigation into the infamous scandal named "Watergate," and the reporters' work became known as some of the most brilliant investigative journalism in history.

As they pursued their investigation, Woodward and Bernstein soon learned that Watergate was no simple burglary. Following what seemed to be an endless series of leads that stretched over two years, the two picked up a trail of money, secrecy, and high-level pressure that led to prominent aides of Richard Nixon, president of the United States, and eventually to Nixon himself. The investigation exposed government corruption and a major cover-up for which many top presidential officials were eventually indicted and sent to prison. And in 1974, facing certain impeachment and removal from office, Richard Nixon resigned as president.

In 1973 Woodward and Bernstein were recognized for their journalistic excellence when *The Washington Post* won the Pulitzer Prize for public service in journalism. In 1974 the two wrote a best-selling account of the Watergate scandal entitled *All the President's Men*, which was eventually made into a movie. And today, almost thirty years after their story was released to the public, the reporters' work serves as an example of how powerful investigative journalism can be.

Another way to gain valuable experience is through internships, which are part-time jobs that offer hands-on training while students attend high school or college. Some internships are paid and some are nonpaid, and most offer academic credits in return for the experience. In high school, internships are valuable as they help students get a real-world look at what a reporter's job is like. For someone in college who has definitely decided on a career as a reporter, one or even several internships are required. Tony Villasana from KDSK-TV in St. Louis, Missouri, coordinates a college internship program that hosts twenty to twenty-five students per school term. He describes the program and its benefits:

> The time each intern spends with us is a win-win situation for the student and the station. The intern is given the opportunity to learn from media professionals in a setting that's unavailable in many colleges and universities. . . . For example, even answering the phone at the assignment desk gives the intern the experience of taking calls that might lead to a story. He or she learns what is potentially newsworthy and how to determine priorities and react accordingly. Interns who do an outstanding job are often referred to news departments seeking entry-level producers, reporters, etc. Interns whose performance is mediocre or marginal quickly learn that their chances of competing are not good. While it may be a bitter pill to swallow, it's an important one in deciding on a career.[14]

Earnings

The first thing beginning reporters discover when job hunting is a wide variance in pay. Reporters' salaries vary based on a number of factors such as geographical location and size of the market. In general, the bigger the market, the bigger the salary. However, reporters who are fresh out of college have the best chances of getting jobs at small local television or radio stations and newspapers. Experience is also an important factor, as reporters with four or five years of hands-on training are considered "seasoned," or more valuable than someone just starting out in the business.

Newspapers typically offer higher starting salaries than radio and television stations. Beginning newspaper reporters usually make from $25,000 per year to more than double that amount at large newspapers in major cities like New York, Boston, or Washington, D.C. Reporters in large cities who have five years of experience can make $75,000 or more per year.

Despite the fact that television reporters have low starting salaries, television is still perceived as the most glamorous and desirable of all media. For those seeking a news career it is also where competition is toughest. Television reporters can start out at very low salaries, as little as $20,000 per year or even less, but with experience their salaries can climb to $100,000, $200,000, or even more. Radio reporters are often the lowest on the pay scale, averaging $19,000 to $35,000.

Reporters who are trying to break into the business often make monetary sacrifices to get the kind of experience and training that will help them be successful in their careers. T.J. Winick, a reporter at WTAE-TV in Pittsburgh, initially accepted a low-paying job and explains why:

> You really have to know what you want to do and then fight for it. . . . I had a choice of taking a $45,000 production job or a $20,000 reporting job in Fort Myers [Florida], and there was never a doubt in my mind about taking the reporting job because that was what I really wanted to do. Even though it wasn't as good financially, I figured if I played my cards right, I would be making that money in a few years anyway.[15]

The Future

Because the news media is such a competitive field reporters can have a tough time finding their first job. The number of new jobs for reporters is not expected to change much in the coming years, with most of the job openings resulting from the need to replace those who leave for retirement or go on to other careers. Consequently, young people who are interested in becoming reporters must study hard in school and pursue every possible opportunity to broaden their knowledge and gain hands-on experience.

Reporters who decide to brave the competition and seek a career in television news soon discover there are far more people who want jobs than there are jobs available. Therefore, beginning television reporters often have to settle for jobs in cities they may never have heard of before, as Filoreto explains:

> Okay, now think about Duluth, Minnesota. Did you draw a blank? Well, try another city. Close your eyes and think about Yakima, Washington. Still nothing? How about Albany, Georgia? Strike three? Why should you ponder these particular cities? Because they are representative of the places you'll

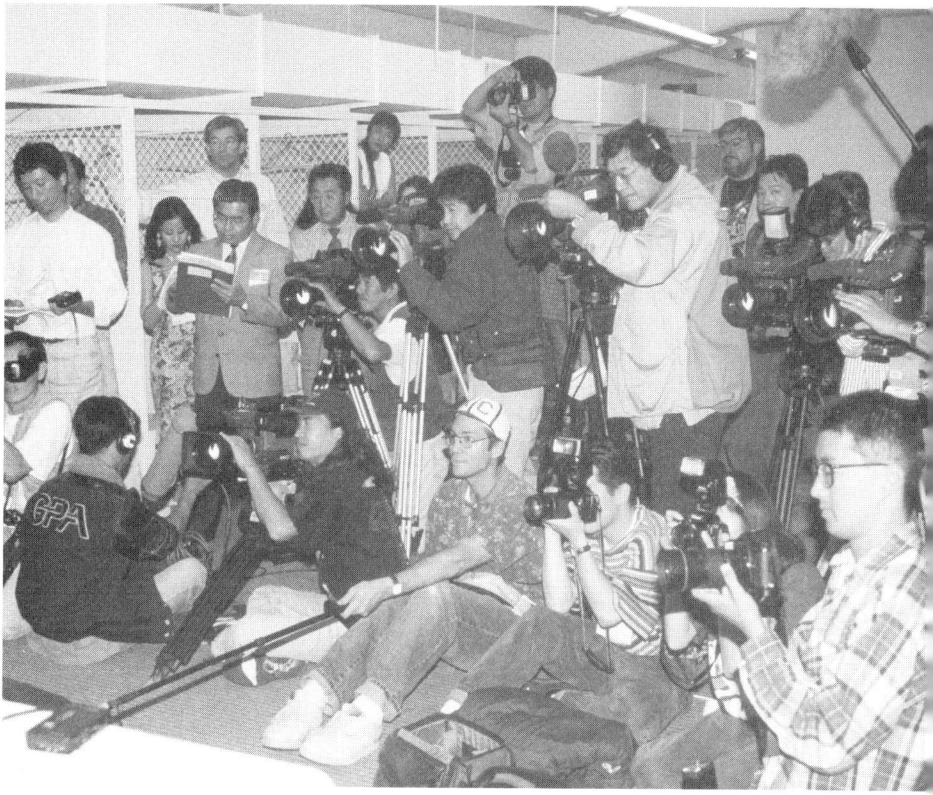

Reporters take part in a press conference. Reporting can be fiercely competitive for those just starting out in the field.

> be applying for your first job in T.V. news. . . . Put away the dreams of starting your career in the Big Apple [New York] or the Windy City [Chicago]. You can cross off Los Angeles and San Francisco too. Even stations in . . . obscure locales like Wichita and Toledo will be a reach for you.[16]

Like television reporters, those who seek jobs in either radio or newspapers also face keen competition. Reporters trying to break into these branches of the media stand the best chance in small suburban areas rather than in large metropolitan cities. Once they gain knowledge and experience they will be more likely to succeed in finding jobs in the bigger markets.

Overall, in spite of the competition, in spite of the unpredictability, in spite of the potential for danger or the built-in stress of the job, most reporters love what they do and would not dream of doing anything else. Mydans describes why:

The main advantage of being a reporter is that it's fun: getting the story and telling it. The main disadvantage is not a disadvantage to those who love the job: it is that being a reporter can consume your time and your energy and your emotions. Yes, there are steady, hard-working, nine-to-five journalistic technocrats, and they can be very good at what they do. But do they have as much fun?[17]

Chapter 2

Photo-journalists

Photojournalists capture moments in time. They are news photographers who tell stories through their cameras, recording events on film so people can see and feel what it was like to experience the event themselves. They provide the pictures, both on television and in print, that bring news stories to life, giving viewers an up close and personal look at people and places all over the world. Photojournalist Carol Guzy explains how powerful these images can be:

> A photograph can be a powerful witness and an eloquent voice for those who have none. Pictures inform, educate, enlighten, captivate and spur governments into action. They are historical documents and poignant reminders of our human frailties. At times they make a difference, though perhaps only a small difference to one person for one moment on one day, but meaningful nevertheless.[18]

As early as the 1800s photojournalists were taking photos of famous people and capturing significant historical events on film. The equipment they used was certainly much more primitive than what is used now, but it is likely these people were lured into their profession for the same reason photojournalists are today: the ability to document history. And although their specialties and areas of the media may vary, all photojournalists have one thing in common: They want their photos to stimulate thoughts and emotions in the people who view them, as photojournalist Nancy Ford explains:

> A great photo happens when a photographer sees a situation unfolding in front of them that evokes an emotion that the photographer feels deep down, in the middle of their chest.

Civil War photographer Alexander Gardner (seated) holds a camera. Photojournalists have been capturing important events on film since the 1800s.

> And in a split second, they then make a conscious choice of exposure, lens, lighting . . . and release the shutter. The film is then processed, scanned, laid out on a page, printed on a press, driven across town to the newspaper carrier who throws it on some guy's porch, who then opens the newspaper and looks down at that photo . . . and if that guy gets the same feeling deep down in the middle of his chest that the photographer did when they viewed the situation in the first place, they have made a great photo.[19]

Seeking the Truth

Photojournalists seek to capture reality through their cameras, so sometimes television footage or photos can be difficult or painful for viewers to see. In 1995, after the bombing of the Murrah Federal Building in Oklahoma City, a freelance photographer captured a heartbreaking moment on film with his photo of tiny Baylee Almon, whose battered body was tenderly cradled in the arms of a firefighter. The famous photo eventually won a Pulitzer Prize, which is an esteemed award given for outstanding artistic achievement. Photojournalist Mark Hertzberg describes how photojournalism must depict reality, whether it involves happiness or tragedy:

> Our cameras are a golden key or a magic passport that open many doors to us. Those of us who shoot pictures . . . are the eyes of the readers. We take you to places you can't go. We show you people and parts of the community you never dreamt exist. We are in the front row when history is made. We're paid to kneel on the sidelines of Packers games. . . . We're paid to bring you countless delightful moments of life. . . . That's the good part. The bad part is that we are also paid to be in the front row when tragedy strikes. We have to be there when people's lives and emotions are ripped apart, as much as we have to be there to celebrate life's great moments.[20]

While a commitment to seeking the truth is important for any media professional, it is especially important for photojournalists. The public may choose not to believe stories they read or hear, but people tend to perceive pictures as reality. Many believe the old saying "the camera never lies"; therefore, photojournalists must show things as they actually are without distorting what the viewer sees. They must photograph only what happens, when it happens. They must not manipulate scenes or shots to make the photos look better or use digital technology to alter photos they have taken. This sometimes can present photojournalists with a dilemma, because they also are artists who care about the quality of their photos; however, their first priority must always be to portray the truth.

Life as a Photojournalist

The responsibilities and duties of photojournalists vary based on which branch of the media they work in. Photojournalists who work for newspapers receive assignments from photo editors, and sometimes they suggest photo stories on their own. Either working alone or in teams with reporters, they go out and shoot their photos, then return to the newspaper to get their film processed and select which photos to use.

Chicago Sun Times photojournalist Jean Lachat says that in her job, each day is completely different from the one before. She calls her office an hour before her shift and often receives a photo assignment. On a normal day, she shoots between two and four assignments involving news, business, features, and/or sports. Once her assignments are complete she goes back to the office, downloads the digital camera disc into the computer, sorts through the images and selects the ones she thinks are best. She then makes color, contrast, and composition corrections and puts her final images into the newspaper's computerized system.

Magazine photojournalists have responsibilities that are similar to those who work for newspapers, but they are often employed on a "freelance" basis, working for themselves and getting paid based on the photos they take. These freelancers supply photos to a variety of different magazines and wire services, and their jobs typically involve a lot of travel. Some magazine photojournalists work for agencies that employ staffs of photojournalists and supply photography to a number of publications.

Since viewers watch television to see what is going on in the news as well as hear about it, television photojournalists play a crucial role. They are the people who travel to the scene of a news event and film it for both live broadcasts and taped broadcasts that are shown at a later time. Photojournalist Carl Filoreto describes the importance of a photojournalist's role in television:

> There wouldn't be much television news without photographers. Everything you see on your cathode-ray tube [television screen] during a newscast that doesn't occur in the studio has been shot by a news photographer somewhere. News photographers are self-contained video factories and can cover news autonomously. A photographer can do a story without a reporter, but not vice versa. It's an essential position.[21]

A Hazardous Occupation

Because it is their job to photograph or film any newsworthy event no matter how risky the situation may be, photojournalists—particularly those who work for news magazines or national television networks—can find themselves in extremely dangerous situations. They are the people behind the cameras, filming the action as it unfolds. If they are in unfriendly territory, such as the scene of a major crime or the frontlines in a war-torn country, their presence can be viewed as an intrusion and reactions toward them can be hostile. Yet photojournalists understand that these risks are a necessary part of the job they have to do, as Guzy explains:

A photojournalist snaps pictures during a battle in the Middle East. Some photojournalists work in countries where turmoil and violence are commonplace.

> I've been screamed at, spit on, occasionally shot at and . . . arrested while on assignment. Slept on roach-ridden floors in distant huts, spent many hours in freezing rains waiting for just one compelling moment, wept at man's endless inhumanity. . . . I have traveled to places I could never have found on a map before—Magunga, Zaire and Kukes, Albania—the list could go on and on. I've experienced cultures and been humbled by the resiliency of people enduring unthinkable hardships. I feel quite blessed to have the privilege of being a voice for these people. And enriched by witnessing the full spectrum of the human condition. It's not always physically or emotionally comfortable by any stretch of the imagination, but certainly soul-enriching.[22]

Photojournalists on location in other countries, particularly those in the volatile Middle East, are aware that turmoil is commonplace and violence can frequently erupt. CNN producer Bruce Conover was in Israel when a riot broke out between Palestinian demonstrators and the Israeli army, and he talks about the dangers he and his crew faced:

> It was clear that we were in the middle of what had turned from the usual daily exchange of rocks and rubber bullets into a full-fledged war zone, with .50-caliber machine gun fire spraying our location and rocket grenades being fired very close to us. . . . The firing was almost continuous at that point. . . . At a lull in the shooting, I raised my head to see where the firing was coming from. At that moment, to my horror, I witnessed a series of small dust-cloud explosions as one of the Israeli soldiers sent some rocket grenades toward a small olive grove about 50 feet ahead of where my cameraman . . . and I were lying.[23]

Danger can also come in the form of natural disasters. Some photojournalists specialize in pursuing weather-related phenomena like hurricanes, tornadoes, and earthquakes, and they actually spend their entire careers traveling to where these natural disasters occur so they can capture them on film. Warren Faidley is a photojournalist from Tucson, Arizona, whose nickname is "The Cyclone Cowboy." His full-time job is to pursue storms and natural disasters, and his images of graphic, sometimes violent weather-related events have been featured in many national publications. Faidley describes the filming of Hurricane Andrew, a fierce storm with 160-mile-per-hour winds: "Hurricanes are likely the most dangerous storms to chase. Instead of shooting the storm from the outside, like tornadoes and lightning, I'm working inside the storm. You cannot simply run away. Once you're committed to a location, you better hope it survives!"[24]

If being a photojournalist involves so much risk, some may wonder why anyone would choose it as a career. Faidley explains that among other things, the challenge is a big part of why he enjoys his job so much:

> Some people might think I'm a "thrill seeker," but I'm not. I don't enjoy risking my life. The simple things many people take for granted are cherished by me because of my experiences. My enjoyment comes from accomplishing a great shot under extreme conditions. It's the challenge I cannot resist and the mystery of never knowing what amazing opportunity will be exposed for a fleeting moment, otherwise lost forever. The scary things that happen are part of my job. I don't enjoy close calls. I do everything as carefully as I can to avoid trouble.[25]

Photojournalism Yesterday and Today

This excerpt is from the Photojournalism Timeline *section of Time Warner's website. The piece gives a glimpse at the history of photojournalism, which dates back to the Civil War, and explains the significant roles that photojournalists play in society—even though their jobs can often lead them into grave danger.*

The history of photojournalism is largely a history of war photography. Among the recorded images most familiar to us are those that depict, in the cold candor of black and white and in lurid color, the brutality of war. Shots of the dead at Gettysburg and Antietam; the famous *Life* magazine shots of doughboys in the trenches of World War I and firebombed cities in World War II; heartrending shots of displaced—and sometimes dismembered—civilians during the Vietnam War. . . .

But photojournalism has done more than just touch our hearts. It has also influenced how we think about and discuss past and current conflicts. Gruesome photos of Civil War casualties helped move the political debate from ideological to practical terms. Heroic images of Allied soldiers and harrowing images of concentration camps ensured the support of the American public during World War II. And the antiwar movement in the 1960s gained considerable momentum because of the close media coverage of violence in Vietnam.

Today, we take for granted that armed conflicts will receive full coverage. Every week, photographs of conflicts in parts of the world we can barely locate—Afghanistan, Libya, Grenada, Algeria, Bosnia, Kosovo, Chechnya, Somalia—are sandwiched between colorful ads in glossy magazines. Battles are televised during prime-time news. Newspapers commit more and more space to photographs, because people want to see the news. If it's true, as many of our leaders have pointed out, that there will never be another world war, it's probably because so many people have such clear visual images of war's absolute brutality. Photojournalists provide those images, often at great risk to themselves.

Who Makes a Good Photojournalist?

Although all photojournalists may not share Faidley's passion for photographing under extreme conditions, they generally do thrive on the challenges and creativity of their profession. They know that photojournalism involves a lot more than just pointing a camera and clicking the shutter or shooting footage with a television camera. It is an art that requires the ability to see things in a creative way, communicating images that attract the interest of viewers, as Filoreto explains: "You are the eyes for your viewers, and it's your job to capture the facts and emotions of a story, while it's happening. . . . Good photographers blend a healthy portion of personal creativity into the mix."[26] And while no two people agree on what makes a "good" photo, generally those that have some sort of profound emotional effect on viewers are the ones that are best remembered.

In addition to being creative the best photojournalists are naturally curious people with a keen interest in different people and places. They must be persistent enough to seek out all sides of a story, while remaining sensitive to the people whom they are photographing. University of Nebraska professor Michael Sherer says that contrary to public perception, most news photographers are sensitive to the feelings of those caught in tragic moments:

> They realize people may be in shock and are often unwilling to be brought into the public eye when tragedy strikes. Photojournalists also know the audience may not be interested in viewing every intimate detail of a tragic situation. A photojournalistic golden rule of treating others as one would wish to be treated is often applied to covering tragic moments. . . . When tragedy strikes, photojournalists confront the difficult fact that television's greatest strength lies in the closeup image. Getting in tight for the most dramatic, emotional and compelling images means that photojournalists must make instant ethical decisions regarding how far to intrude into the lives of others. . . . The ugly side of life with all its tragedy and sorrow takes a toll on news photographers. It is not uncommon to hear stories of photojournalists feeling empathy with victims of tragedy and sorrow.[27]

Another quality photojournalists need is the ability to think quickly and adapt to any situation because their jobs can change day by day and even minute by minute. By the very nature of the profession they have chosen, photojournalists must learn to expect the unexpected and be prepared to cope with anything. For instance, one day they may be photographing a local high school football team and the next day a serious multiple-car pileup on the highway. Some assignments will be more appealing than others, but photojournalists must complete their assignments regardless of the circumstances.

In addition, as with any media professional, photojournalists' assignments and schedules vary constantly based on what happens in the news. That means pressing deadlines are a fact of life, as are long, often erratic hours—a workday that is typically eight or nine hours can grow to double that amount if there is important news that must be covered.

How to Get There

A career in photojournalism generally requires a four-year college degree but most experts say the degree does not necessarily have to be in a journalism-related field. Bradley Wilson, executive director of the Newspaper Press Photographers Association, says few employers require a degree in journalism or photojournalism and some even believe that a degree in another field can give photojournalists deeper insight into the world around them.

Washington, D.C., photojournalist George Bridges says the most important thing is to get as broad an education as possible: "Study things that will interest you besides photography and stay up-to-date on current events. In this job you will meet, and spend time talking with, everyone from workers picking crops for a few dollars a day to corporate chiefs earning $100 million-plus a year and just about everyone in between."[28] No matter what aspiring photojournalists choose to major in, it helps to study as many journalism- and photography-related subjects as possible, as well as art, writing, media ethics and law, and computerized photo editing.

Hands-on experience is essential for anyone who desires to break into the field of photojournalism, and there are many things young people can do to prepare long before reaching college age. One important skill is to develop a good eye for photography by making it a hobby. Taking pictures of family and friends or happenings around the neighborhood or town can help develop skill with a camera. Veteran photojournalist Anthony "Val" Mazzenga says that aspiring photographers should focus on getting experience and not worry too much about what they are taking pictures of. "Shoot as much as possible, everything. Shoot every event there is. . . . Just build your eye. . . . The whole trick is to learn photography before you get into photojournalism."[29]

Summer or part-time work for a newspaper or magazine provides valuable experience as does working at a local television station. Job shadowing or mentor programs, which involve spending time with photojournalists while they work, is an excellent way to get a first-hand look at the job. Basically, young people interested in pursuing a photojournalism career should seek out every possible opportunity to get experience in the field.

One or more internships are almost always required for photojournalism careers. They provide aspiring photojournalists in high school and/or college with hands-on training in a real media setting, either at a print publication or a television station. The internships can be paid or unpaid and usually earn students academic credits when they have been completed. In addition to getting real-world experience, students who do internships may also have the advantage of a "foot in the door" with a potential employer who has had a chance to see how they perform and may offer them permanent jobs later as a result of this experience.

Photographers on the scene at a mountain biking competition. Young people interested in photojournalism can gain valuable experience photographing local events.

Lachat was interested in photojournalism from a very young age, and she talks about the experience leading up to her current position at the *Chicago-Sun Times:*

> I loved taking photographs of my friends and family as a kid. I worked for my high school paper as a photographer and photo editor. Then I went to [University of Illinois], where I wanted to work for the student paper because I had fun doing it in high school. I started at the *Daily Illini* the first week of freshman year as a staff photographer, and I fell in love with the job. . . . It was such a blast! Also, the DI, as we so fondly call it, was full of talented writers and photographers. I learned by doing from a great group of people.[30]

While in college, students should work on building their portfolios, which are not merely photo albums but a collection of their best photography work. These samples can come from photojournalism class assignments, work performed during internships, or photography the students have shot on their own time. The portfolio is an important factor in helping a photojournalist get his or her first job, as a potential employer can see firsthand the student's talent and creativity with a camera.

Earnings

People who choose to pursue a photojournalism career usually choose it because of their passion, not because they seek a huge salary. The reality is that photojournalism often pays a relatively low salary for the amount of work involved, as Ford explains: "Students always ask if there is money to be made in photojournalism. Sure, anyone can make money in any career, depending how you approach it I guess. But like I always say: If you are planning to pursue a career in photojournalism, then you should make sure that journalism is in your blood and that you love it, because frankly, you are NOT going to get rich doing it."[31]

The amount of money photojournalists earn is closely related to their knowledge and proven talent with a camera, which is why it is important to get as much experience as possible before seeking a job. In 2000 television photojournalists' salaries averaged around $30,000 per year, ranging from a low of $13,000 to over $125,000. Print photojournalists' salaries averaged from just under $20,000 to $65,000 per year. In both print and broadcast photojournalism, salaries vary based on the geographic location and the size of the publication or television station.

Some photojournalists are employed full time and also do freelance photography on the side. And an increasing number of photojournalists, possibly as many as half, are self-employed as freelancers. These professionals negotiate their own rates and get paid by the individual project, so they are not paid a regular yearly salary. Their rates vary—some photojournalists charge by the picture, and some charge based on a daily fee known as a "day rate." *The Christian Science Monitor,* a prominent Boston newspaper, pays its freelance photographers a "half-day rate" of $175 plus miscellaneous expenses.

Future Outlook

The photojournalism field is extremely popular and attracts many hopeful applicants every year, so competition is tough and is expected to get tougher in the future. Those who succeed at obtaining full-time positions in print or broadcast photojournalism are likely to be those with the best education and widest breadth of experience. Also, because photography technology is changing rapidly, in the coming years it will be necessary for photojournalists to be able to understand new digital technology and be comfortable using it.

Television is the most competitive medium but it is also the most popular with the public, so it employs the most people. This popularity, combined with the rapid growth of cable and other pay television services, indicates that television offers the most potential for aspiring photojournalists. In fact, according to the U.S. Department of Labor, the need for television photojournalists is expected to increase by as much as 20 percent through the year 2008.

Newspapers, however, are a different story. Their popularity has been declining over the past ten years, so the need for newspaper photojournalists is not likely to increase much in the future. However, wire services like the Associated Press and United Press International, which supply photography to newspapers all over the world, will continue to need skilled photojournalists who can shoot digital images of national and world events. Also, because of the growing number of online newspapers and magazines, there will continue to be a demand for print photojournalists who can provide digital images for the Web.

The Coveted Pulitzer Prize

Photojournalists are artists, and most artists are motivated by recognition of their work. In the world of photojournalism there is no greater honor than to be the recipient of the Pulitzer Prize, which is the most coveted of all journalistic awards.

In the late nineteenth century, a skillful newspaper publisher named Joseph Pulitzer stood out in the world of journalism. Pulitzer was known for his boldness and the passion he had for his profession, which was evident in the long hours he worked and his personal interest in every detail of his newspaper. He considered his paper the champion of the public and frequently ran investigative articles and editorials that attacked government corruption, wealthy tax dodgers, and gamblers.

Pulitzer died in 1911, and in his will he made provisions for the establishment of the Pulitzer Prizes as rewards for excellence in journalism, letters and drama, and education. The first Pulitzer Prizes were given out in 1917. Since that time the Pulitzer Prize has been expanded from the original journalism awards to include photography, musical composition, cartoons, fiction and nonfiction writing, plays, and poetry. No matter what the category, any person who holds a Pulitzer Prize is the recipient of one of the most distinguished awards in existence today.

Each year more than two thousand entries are submitted in the Pulitzer Prize competitions, and only twenty-one awards are normally made. The awards are the culmination of a process that begins early in the year with the appointment of judges who serve on twenty separate juries, and who are asked to make three nominations in each of the twenty-one categories. The awards are given out each May at Columbia University.

All photojournalists have their own personal reasons for choosing what they do for a living. But they all share a belief in the power of photography to capture emotions and feelings on camera, resulting in images that make a difference in the world. This is what motivates them—even when their hours are long, their schedules are impossible, and their jobs can be dangerous, as Guzy explains:

Photography has enriched my life with a tapestry of experiences. I've looked up close at the anguish of conflict, the thrill of revolution, the rapture of liberation. . . . It is said that when you make a photo, you take a piece of the soul. It is indeed a privilege for journalists to bear witness to history, both the major news events and the small moments of

A photographer carries a girl out of harm's way. Photojournalists find satisfaction in confronting a variety of people and experiences.

humanity that provide a record of our time. But it is haunting to voyage into so many different souls. What we behold clings to us and changes us. We see people's most intimate moments—their joys and sorrows, their triumphs and tragedies. . . . There is satisfaction in hearing your work has made someone angry, then made them think, then made them act. Each of us leaves behind what we've done and who we've been.[32]

Chapter 3

Television Anchors

Of all the many people involved in bringing the news to the public, television anchors are the most visible. Theirs are the faces viewers see when they turn on their televisions to watch the news, and they are the ones who are considered the "stars" of the news programs.

There are a number of different types of news anchors. National anchors who work for national television networks like NBC, ABC, CBS, and CNN are the most famous because the news they broadcast is shown in cities all over the country and in other parts of the world. *Wall Street Journal* television critic Robert Goldberg writes about three famous anchors: "They could be members of the family, their faces are so familiar to us. . . . Who doesn't know Rather, Brokaw and Jennings? Collectively, these three top journalists who anchor the national evening news are among the most influential media figures in the country."[33]

Local television stations all over the country have their own staffs of anchors. These people often work in pairs, called co-anchors, and each anchor team is responsible for a certain newscast; for example, one team may cover the morning and noontime news, and another team may cover the evening and late night news. Local stations also have specialized anchors who have their own areas of responsibility such as news, weather, and sports.

Looking Out from the Anchor's Desk

Whenever anchors are live on the air, they are in a broadcast studio. The viewing public sees a spacious well-furnished room in which the anchor desk is the focal point. That is a made-for-television illusion however, as in many studios that desk is the *only* piece of furniture. The floors are concrete, and there is carpeting only where it is visible on-camera, under the anchors' desk. The whole studio is crowded with cameras and computer equipment, and almost every inch of the ceiling is covered with a veritable jungle of cords and lights and sound insulation.

Someone sitting at the anchor desk is faced with television cameras on the right, the middle, and the left. On top of each camera an essential piece of equipment is mounted called the "TelePrompTer," a device that helps news anchors look like they have memorized stories by prompting them with words they can read while on the air. John McQuiston, a sports anchor for WTVQ-TV in Lexington, Kentucky, describes what an anchor experiences while in front of the camera: "A good anchor or reporter calmly and confidently tells you what's going on no matter what chaos may be going on around him or her . . . there is nothing natural about talking to a box with words scrolling up before your eyes while wearing a small speaker in your ear in a room only slightly less lit than direct sunlight on the planet Mercury."[34]

The chaos McQuiston refers to could be anything from late-breaking news that must interrupt regular programming, to sound or transmission problems with the recorded news segments. Or it simply could be the normal day-to-day activities of a news station, which can often be quite hectic simply because of the nature of the news.

Overall, the making of a news program is an interesting event. In the minutes before a newscast is scheduled to go on the air the studio is alive with activity as people bark words like "check, check, check!" to test the sound system, and the anchors read over their scripts and request close-up camera shots to check their appearances. They attach small microphones to their lapels called Lavalieres, and then it is time for the news to begin. The camera operator says "thirty seconds left," then "five, four, three, two . . .," gives a hand signal that there is one second left, and the anchors are live on the air talking to thousands, or even millions, of viewers.

During a broadcast anchors follow a program plan that has been predetermined by a producer. In a thirty-minute newscast time is allotted for live news by the anchors and prerecorded news segments featuring on-the-scene reporters as well as commercials, sports, and weather reports. To keep the anchors on schedule, producers can communicate with them through hidden microphones throughout

How a TelePrompTer Works

When news anchors are on camera, they must look as natural as possible and appear as if they are reciting the news from memory. Years ago anchors depended on cue cards to read the news. Now they use an innovative device called the TelePrompTer.

A TelePrompTer displays scripts several lines at a time, which scroll along like the credits at the end of a movie. It is mounted on a camera and resembles a television, with the screen facing upward toward the ceiling. Just behind the screen is a piece of glass that reflects the words so the anchors can read them. This glass acts like a mirror, and since mirrors reflect backward, the letters on the monitor must be backward so the words appear normal to the anchors as they read them.

Because maintaining eye contact with viewers is necessary for anchors to appear believable and sincere, the TelePrompTer is designed so the camera lens is directly behind the glass. That means as the anchors read the script, they are actually looking into the camera—and directly into the eyes of their audience.

This vital piece of equipment is controlled by the TelePrompTer operator, who sits at a computer terminal behind the TelePrompTer. The operator has a lot of responsibility, as he or she must call up the scripts in the correct order and sometimes make last-minute changes. TelePrompTer operators often control how fast the words slide up the screen so the anchors can read them comfortably; however, at some stations anchors have their own set of controls. During the newscast, TelePrompTer operators must remain focused on their work because what they do has a significant impact on how the anchors perform on camera.

TelePrompTers (background) help television anchors recite the news.

the broadcast. Juliet Dragos, news anchor for WZZM-TV in Grand Rapids, Michigan, says this can sometimes be difficult: "While I'm on the air, I have a tiny speaker in my ear so I can hear my producer if he needs to talk to me. Sometimes he's talking at the same time I'm talking, so it can be challenging to pay attention to what he's saying while I'm saying something entirely different. However, in time anchors just get used to that."[35]

Being Real

Something else news anchors must get used to is the importance of their role to the public. Whether national or local, anchors are the people who talk to the viewing audience day after day, week after week, so they must be both credible and believable. Terri Ouellette, anchor of the morning television news program *Good Morning Arizona*, explains her sense of responsibility to the viewers who watch her: "You always have to keep in mind that people not only listen to what you say, but believe what you say, so you have to be careful and take that responsibility very seriously."[36]

Because their credibility with the public is so important, news anchors must appear natural on camera so they are seen as real people, not actors. They must also be sincere and convey a sense of caring to viewers. Virginia Sherwood, formerly an ABC anchor who now coaches news professionals throughout the country, says anchors must care enough to present the news in the best way possible. She explains:

> It bothers me today when I see anchors or reporters who seem to be playing a "role" . . . rather than concentrating on the story, and reaching out and sharing that story with us. Your job is to inform, to explain, to talk to us, to educate us, if necessary. The best thing you can do is forget yourself because you think so much of that story and then the real self will come through. What you do is explain. You talk to us. The camera is not a camera, it's people. . . . Forget about the phony head movements and the vocal acrobatics or the vocal games which say, "Look at me. Listen to me." Rather than, "Listen to this story. It's something you need to know, you ought to know, you want to know."[37]

However, in spite of the fact that news anchors must seem natural to their viewers, there are times when being calm and poised is difficult, if not impossible. This is especially true when the subject matter is alarming or tragic; yet even in these situations, anchors must do their best to hide their own emotions as they broadcast the news. Veteran anchorman Walter Cronkite had the unfortunate and sad task of announcing to the world that President John F. Kennedy had been shot. Later in his broadcast he had to present the shocking news that the president had died. He describes how he felt as he went on the air:

> It is an interesting thing about us newspeople. We are much like doctors and nurses and firemen and police. In the midst of tragedy, our professional drive takes over and dominates our emotions. We move almost like automatons to get the job done. The time for an emotional reaction must wait. I was doing fine in that department until it was necessary to pronounce the words "President Kennedy died at 1 P.M. Central Standard Time an hour ago. . . ." The words stuck in my throat. A sob wanted to replace them. A gulp or two quashed the sob, which metamorphosed into tears forming in the corners of my eyes. I fought back the emotion and regained my professionalism, but it was touch and go there for a few seconds before I could continue.[38]

Walter Cronkite (left) interviews President John F. Kennedy in September 1963. Cronkite had the sad task of announcing Kennedy's death just two months later.

Anchors spend much of their time working outside of the studio, holding interviews that are taped for later news programs.

Dragos says that when the subject matter is difficult she has to remind herself that she has a job to do, and that job is to stay composed and inform her viewers about the news. "Everything can be falling down around you but the audience depends on you to give them the feeling that things are going to be okay. I have to do my best to let them know what is happening, while trying to keep my own feelings from interfering. Sometimes that isn't easy. But that's my job."[39]

A News Anchor's Day

News anchors are indeed important to their viewers, but they are sometimes perceived as people who work only a few hours a day posing in front of a television camera. The truth, however, is that the time anchors spend on the air is but a small part of their total workload. Their schedules are full, their days are busy, and they often work long hours, including many weekends and holidays. Most anchors help write scripts for the news, and they also write and anchor the short news "teases" that are aired during regular programming in the hours prior to newscasts. They hold interviews with people, both inside and outside of the station, which are taped for later news programs. Because of their celebrity status, anchors make regular personal appearances at special events or take part in various activities that show their involvement in the community. Many also have reporter duties, which means they work on news packages or cover out-of-town events.

News anchors have schedules that vary based on when their news is on the air, and those who broadcast the early morning news are typically up and at the station long before dawn. Toby Cook, a news anchor for FOX-TV in Kansas City, is up each morning at 3:00 A.M. and at work by 3:45. He spends his first hour at the studio looking over news scripts for the day, then heads for the makeup room. (Television studio lights generate a great deal of heat, so both men and women wear makeup to get rid of facial disparities and absorb excess moisture.) Cook is on the air at 5:00 A.M. with his morning broadcast, which runs for two hours. When he is finished with his news segment he goes out into the city and reports live stories until 9:00. Cook admits that his schedule is difficult: "You don't have a normal life, you work weird hours and holidays, get up in the middle of the night, go to bed early and are away from your family a lot."[40]

Early morning anchors who broadcast from stations on the other side of the world have responsibilities and schedules similar to their U.S. counterparts. Toko Takeuchi has been co-anchor of *Ohayo Nippon* (Good Morning Japan) for the past five years. She starts her day at 2:30 A.M., arriving at the studio by 4:00 to prepare for the program that is on the air from 7:00 until 8:15 A.M. Like most early morning news programs, *Ohayo Nippon* focuses on news that happens during the night. Takeuchi says that most of the program has already been planned by 5:00 A.M., but breaking news can come in that throws the schedule off and creates challenges for the news team. One example was a hostage crisis at the Japanese embassy in Peru: "That happened in the morning our time just as we were about to go to air. We weren't sure what was happening. Shots were heard, smoke was seen and it was coming to us live. It's hard when the news comes in bit by bit because it doesn't give the media much of a chance to analyze it before going to air."[41]

Evening news anchors have the same basic responsibilities as morning anchors, the only difference being their schedules. Dragos is anchor for both the 6:00 and 11:00 P.M. newscasts. After making community appearances in the afternoon, she arrives at the station at 4:30 and begins her "pre-production" preparation for her first newscast of the evening. She studies the scripts given to her by the

The Role of the TV Meteorologist

Most television stations employ several different types of anchors who host their news programs. One type is a "weather anchor," who is often a trained meteorologist, and is responsible for interpreting and analyzing weather-related data. The meteorologist then passes this information on to the viewing public in the form of a weather report.

TV meteorologists have a variety of sophisticated, expensive equipment at their disposal. Many stations have their own radar systems called "Doppler" radar, which can pinpoint the strongest thunderstorms (including possible tornadoes), heaviest rain, and strongest winds. Doppler radar can also project the path of a storm so stations can estimate when it will arrive at a particular location. In an article in the *Kansas City Star*, Gary Lezak, meteorologist with Kansas City station KSHB-TV, was quoted as saying that because of its accuracy in detecting inclement weather "Doppler radar is probably the most important tool for severe-weather detection." In addition to their own radar equipment, TV stations also have access to the National Weather Service's powerful Nexrad radar.

Many TV stations also have separate weather-reporting stations that are located around their cities, with each of these reporting current conditions at its location. In addition, some have "skyview" cameras that help monitor weather conditions. And technology is constantly being developed that will help meteorologists be even more exact in reporting weather conditions in the future.

In the course of their jobs, TV meteorologists have to make decisions about what to report and when. If there is no severe weather, they will just give their regular weather report at the end of a news broadcast. However, if a tornado, hurricane, or other severe storm is approaching, they must make decisions about interrupting regular programming to give listeners the warning. Meteorologist Bryan Busby of Kansas City's KMBC-TV told the *Kansas City Star* how imperative it is for someone in his job to remain calm in these situations. "If you're on a plane," he says, "and the flight attendant has sweat on the brow and a quivering voice to tell you that everything is all right, you're not going to believe that message. The last thing you need is for us to look excited and unnerved by what we're reporting."

producer, and sometimes writes her own scripts. At 5:30 she is on the air with a short promotion for the 6:00 news, then she spends another twenty minutes looking over her scripts. After fixing her hair and makeup (contrary to popular opinion many anchors do this themselves) she is back on the air from 6:00 until 6:30. When that program is finished, the process starts all over again in preparation for the 11:00 news. At 11:30 P.M. Dragos's news broadcasts are finished for the day, but her workday is far from over. She receives hundreds of e-mails and letters each week and usually answers them after her last newscast. She also reports one news package a week, which involves quite a bit of work. As for when she finally can go home, Dragos says that varies: "On a good day I might get out of here by 1:00 A.M., but that's never guaranteed. Whenever the news changes, my schedule has to change with it. That's just the nature of this business."[42]

A Glamorous Profession?

No matter how hard they work or how busy their schedules are, news anchors are sometimes perceived as little more than professional actors who do the least amount of work while getting the most attention and highest salaries. While that may be the case in some major markets, the truth is that most news anchors' jobs are not nearly as glamorous as people often think. Yes, they may be viewed as celebrities, but that does not mean their jobs are easy. In fact, the job of anchor can be stressful, emotionally draining, and tiring. There is constant pressure to achieve higher ratings than other stations as well as retain credibility with viewers. Plus, there is an abundance of young, talented people who want nothing more than to sit in the anchor's chair, so there is always a fear of being replaced.

Another aspect of a news anchor's job that is anything but glamorous is the long hours they often work. After shooting *Good Morning Arizona* for five hours each day, Ouellette works on promotions for the next day's show, writes and tapes segments for future programs, and a few days a week she works on another show she hosts called *Home with Terri-O*. She says some days can be long and exhausting, with twelve- or thirteen-hour days.

Part of the perceived glamour of an anchor's job is the celebrity appearances they make at fund-raisers and community events. However, anchors are constantly inundated with invitations for these activities and by taking on too much, their days can become overloaded and very long. Dragos explains:

It's very hard to say no, but there are people who burn out in this business because they try to cram too much in. I've learned through experience that I can't say yes to everything I'm asked to do. For example, I can't schedule a community event at 9:00 A.M. because by the time I'm on the air with the 11:00 P.M. news, I'm exhausted and looking pretty haggard. It's important that I be involved in the community and these activities are a priority with me. But my first priority has to be doing my job well. I owe that to my viewers. So for me, as for most anchors, the key is maintaining a balance.[43]

The Road to the Top

Even though news anchor jobs may not be as glamorous as many people think, the perception is still one of glamour. Therefore, the job of news anchor is considered the most prestigious, most coveted position in television. It almost always requires a four-year college degree, and according to a survey sponsored by the Radio-Television News Directors Foundation, most television news directors prefer degrees from colleges and universities that give students hands-on training in broadcast news. There are approximately 450 colleges around the country that offer journalism and broadcast journalism programs; three of the most well-known and respected are Columbia University, University of Missouri, and Northwestern University.

NBC anchor Tom Brokaw at the Rose Parade in Pasadena, California.

However, having a degree is certainly not a ticket to a news anchor position for recent college graduates. They have to work their way up from the bottom, and that takes years of experience and hard work. While in college, Ouellette says she "worked for anybody who would let me come in and sit and look over their shoulder, and I worked for many years without getting paid just because I was trying to learn. It's all about paying your dues." One of her jobs was working at a small local cable television station as an entertainment reporter. She says she put in countless hours for no pay, but she does not regret the experience. "I cut my teeth there. I learned so much about being on camera and how to produce a package."[44]

After finishing college and completing one or more internships, almost all anchors start out as production assistants or entry-level reporters in small markets, where they gain invaluable knowledge and experience about a news career. It is this experience that can eventually lead to an anchor position. Ouellette offers this advice to anyone who dreams of eventually becoming an anchor: "When you have a goal, you have to realize that there are baby steps that you have to take in order to get to that goal, and sometimes those baby steps are not fun. Sometimes, they are very difficult, and sometimes even painful. But you have to gain as much experience as possible. It's all about gaining some sort of knowledge and experience."[45]

Most veteran news anchors agree that the focus must *not* be on the anchor position itself but rather on building knowledge and gaining experience. NBC News foreign affairs correspondent Andrea Mitchell says she has little patience for people who tell her "I want to be an anchor." She explains:

> This is not a career goal. Tell me you want to be a journalist and I will do anything that I can to help guide you to a reasonable path. But, don't start out thinking you want to be an anchor. The best anchors, as Brokaw, Rather, Jennings, and Jim Lehrer have proved time and time again, are the best journalists. These are people who can handle breaking news, who can anchor conventions, who can cover politics, who can anchor a debate, and do an informed interview without having somebody whispering in their ear what the next question ought to be. So get it all learned. Get the foundations learned, building block by building block. And don't think that you can just leap to the top of celebrity without having done the fundamentals.[46]

Earnings and the Future

Just as someone should not enter the television field expecting to become an anchor overnight, he or she must also not expect a huge

Anchor Dan Rather (right) interviews President Bill Clinton. Famous anchors can earn annual salaries in the millions.

salary as a beginning anchor. Earnings for news anchors are most often influenced by the size of the market in which they are located. In small- to medium-sized markets anchors usually average from $25,000 to $50,000 per year, while those in larger markets can earn from $65,000 to over $1 million per year. Experience is also a huge factor in news anchors' salaries, as beginning anchors earn significantly less than those with more years spent behind the anchor desk.

Famous anchors like Katie Couric of NBC's *Today* show or Peter Jennings of ABC News earn annual salaries in the millions, but these high-profile jobs are rare. Just as aspiring athletes dream of becoming Michael Jordan or aspiring actors dream of becoming Leonardo DiCaprio, most everyone interested in a television career dreams of someday being a famous anchor. The reality, however, is that very few actually make it to the top.

According to the Federal Communications Commission, there are nearly seventeen hundred television stations in the United States. Each of these stations employs a number of news professionals like reporters, producers, photojournalists, and others, with the stations in larger markets employing the most. However, the number

Men vs. Women: Are the Rules the Same?

It is a fact that most people who appear on camera are at least somewhat physically attractive. This does not mean an anchor has to look like a beauty queen or famous actor, but looks and good grooming do matter to the viewing public. The question is, do the same rules apply to women's appearances as men's, or are women held to higher standards? Richard Threlkeld, a correspondent with CBS News, believes that women in television are held to a higher standard than men, as he explains in the book *Women in Television News Revisited:*

"I think it's much more difficult if you're a woman than for a man. And I think that's always been true. If you're a man, you look distinguished as you get older, and if you're a woman, the perception is you just look older. . . . I think that the prejudice against women is greater, at least in on-air roles, as they get older, and all you have to do is look around to find the evidence of that. David Brinkley is still on television, and Mike Wallace is still on television, and a lot of the women that we know . . . aren't."

However, even though the standards for women anchors are still higher, there are signs that things may be changing for the better. In the past, women in their forties were rarely seen on television. Now, famous middle-aged female anchors like Connie Chung, Diane Sawyer, Leslie Stahl, Jane Pauley, and Barbara Walters are still extremely successful. In fact, more and more female television anchors around the country are remaining in their careers well past the age of forty, and this is a significant change from twenty or even ten years ago.

Chung discusses this shift in attitude toward women in *Women in Television News Revisited:* "I think that's the one area that women have made some very healthy progress—thanks to Barbara Walters, who will be on the air until she's 202 because she looks terrific and she is the hardest worker and the most successful person, I think, in television news. . . . And because she has created her niche in the television news industry, I think all of us will be able to stay on the air longer. Those of us who are in the next generation . . . are in our fifties now and we are lasting very nicely."

of anchor jobs is outweighed by the number of people who want these jobs, as stated in the U.S. Department of Labor's *Occupational Outlook Handbook:*

> Competition for jobs as announcers [news anchors] will be keen because the broadcasting field attracts many more job seekers than there are jobs. . . . Interns usually receive preference for available positions. Because competition for ratings is so intense in major metropolitan areas, large stations will continue to seek announcers who have proven that they can attract and retain a large audience. . . . Employment of announcers is expected to decline through 2010 due to the lack of growth of new . . . television stations.[47]

The road to becoming a news anchor is one paved with years of hard work as well as hard knocks. Yet people who have achieved the coveted role of anchor love what they do. Theirs is a profession that allows them to be in the limelight, in front of the camera, conveying the news to their viewers. Dragos shares her feelings about her career:

> I love what I do, and my favorite time is when I'm on the air. It takes dozens of people to create a newscast and when I'm in front of the camera, that's the culmination of what our team has worked so hard for all day. I don't think of myself as a celebrity—I'm just a person who does the news. I always remember that the viewers who tune in to our program night after night, who invite us into their homes, don't have to do that. They choose to do that.[48]

Susan King, who spent over twenty years working her way up from what she calls "a glorified secretary" position to an anchor job at WJLA-TV in Washington, D.C., offers this advice to young people who aspire to be news anchors:

> To get started you'll probably have to bleed, and they'll make you bleed. Be persistent. Work as hard as you can and have no illusions. . . . I have absolutely no regrets from my career. I love the business of journalism. I think it is the people's trust. And it can be a fascinating way to be a player in your society and never compromise your values. I think true talent and quality does survive.[49]

Chapter 4

Broadcast Producers

Producers are not seen on television or heard on the radio, but without them news programs could not exist. They are behind-the-scenes people who are in charge of each newscast, and they are vital to the success of any programming. Producers decide what stories will be included in each news program and which news stories are the most important. They are responsible for the overall "flow," or pacing, of a news program; how the entire news program is structured and how many times the anchors are on camera.

Perhaps the easiest way to understand a producer's function is to consider the definition of the word "produce," which is "to give being, form, or shape to." That is exactly what broadcast producers do: They determine exactly how each show will look and sound. Every day when viewers watch a half-hour news program on television, or when people listen to a radio show, the structure of these programs is meticulously developed by producers, based on what they believe is most important and relevant to the viewing or listening audience. Broadcast production expert Valerie Hyman explains the producer's role: "What a privilege it is to produce news programs, and what a challenge. To decide what goes in and what stays out, to influence reporters and photojournalists as they work, to determine how to present stories most effectively, to shape the way news programs are promoted."[50]

Types of Producers and What They Do

Most all broadcast producers have some level of management responsibility, which varies based on how high they are in the station's hierarchy as well as the size of the station. For example, at a small- or medium-sized station there may be one or two producers who "wear many hats," meaning they are responsible for all programming tasks. This could include developing the overall choreography for programs, determining program content, and supervising the development of all programs from start to finish. These people may also perform tasks like writing scripts, monitoring technical equipment to ensure that it runs smoothly, and managing budgets. In general, the smaller the station, the wider the variety of a producer's tasks.

Large stations often have many different levels of producers. "Executive producers" are top-level managers who have ultimate responsibility for everything that is broadcast by a station. These people are responsible for the "big picture," which means they work with station management on long-range planning, develop station programming budgets, and implement/monitor station policies. Executive producers usually do not get involved in day-to-day programming tasks; instead, they manage the work of other producers who handle these tasks. The executive producer is a powerful individual among station staff—but along with this power comes a great

Broadcast producers, like those seen here, decide how a program will look and sound.

deal of pressure because he or she usually bears the blame if anything goes wrong. For instance, if the station's ratings are poor, the executive producer is likely to be held responsible. Executive producer Mike Andrews from WRCB in Chattanooga, Tennessee, explains the pressure someone in his position typically faces: "You have to watch out for the power play squeeze—people above and below trying to influence you and your decisions. It's your butt on the line and you can't blame anyone else."[51]

Executive producers often have a team of producers who report to them. At the largest stations there may be twenty or more people who have the word "producer" on their business cards. Their actual titles may be "line producers," "show producers," "associate producers," or in many cases just "producers." These people handle daily programming activities and decisions, and while their actual titles may vary from station to station, their responsibilities are quite similar. For instance, producers are often assigned to develop and produce one or two of the station's programs, and they spend much of their time coordinating the activities of other team members in the newsroom who work on these programs. They act as advisers to station management to keep them informed about what is going on at their station as well as out on the street. They constantly monitor the competition's newscasts on television and on the radio. They gather news and write scripts and also edit and approve scripts that are written by reporters and anchors. They act as coaches for production assistants to help them develop their job skills and knowledge. They listen to the contributions and opinions of reporters, photojournalists, and anchors, constantly answering questions and solving problems.

In essence, producers are the ones who pull together all the people, processes, and everything else necessary to make a station's programs come to life. Nashville news director Al Tompkins sums this up: "Producing is the glue that holds the newsroom together. You set the tone. You regulate style. You shape content. Wars have been fought over the struggle of who would get the authority that you hold daily."[52]

In addition to working at local television and radio stations, some producers work for national networks. NBC, CBS, and ABC are all national television networks based in New York City; CNN is based in Atlanta. National Public Radio (NPR) is located in

A producer (center) receives input from a production assistant. Producers coordinate the station's daily programming activities.

Washington, D.C. These networks employ large staffs of producers who have essentially the same responsibilities as those at local stations, but are usually more specialized—like producers who work at large local stations, these people are typically responsible for developing one or two news programs instead of an entire day's programming.

A Typical Television Producer's Day

A television studio never sleeps, and producers' work schedules are based on which programs they are responsible for. Ed Poplin, who spent five years as a producer at television stations in San Luis Obispo, California, and Denver, Colorado, says his day started around 7:30 A.M. when he met with the overnight crew to determine what had happened the night before. If there was a major crime committed during the night, such as a homicide or robbery, he assigned someone to follow up with the police department to get the details. He reviewed tapes of news that had been featured by other area stations and looked over the morning newspaper headlines to get an idea of what the competition had reported. He also reviewed the "news feeds" (taped news footage) from the station's national network affiliate and went over the news that came in from the wire services, such as Associated Press and United Press International.

Poplin then met with the news director, assignment editor, and several reporters to discuss the news of the day. These morning meetings are typical of most all television stations because that is when decisions are made about the day's programming and reporters are assigned accordingly. Poplin says the idea is to put the station's resources where they will be the most productive and cover the most important news. He explains:

> What most people don't realize is that the amount of news that can fit in a 30-minute broadcast is roughly the same amount that's on the front page of a newspaper. You can't possibly cover everything—you don't have enough people and you don't have enough time. So you have to make decisions about what gets reported and what doesn't. Do you need to send a reporter and a cameraman? A reporter and no cameraman? Or maybe a cameraman but no reporter? The idea is to put station resources where they can do the most good.[53]

While reporters were out covering the day's stories, Poplin developed the "rundown," or the order of how all stories would be broadcast during a particular program. The rundown is an extremely important responsibility for any producer, as it is a detailed plan that guides everyone on the news team and includes exact times for each segment of the news broadcast. Author Ted White tells about the rundown's importance: "Some nights, I know, producers wish they could just toss everything in the air and put it in the show the way it falls down. Unfortunately, it doesn't work that way. A lot of thought must go into the arrangement of stories in the newscast, and this organization is expressed in the rundown."[54] Producers are constantly under pressure to get the rundown right. Obviously the more experienced they are, the more likely they will make the best decisions about programming.

Once Poplin completed the rundown and approved the scripts written by reporters, he distributed them to the anchors and director so they could have time to review them before the news went on the air. He also did one final check of the "cumulative time" for the broadcast. He explains the importance of this:

Timing Is Everything

In radio and television news everything is dictated by timing. Without exception the news begins at the same time every day, so the second the anchor goes on the air, the lead story in broadcast news must be ready. This lead story is included in the producer's rundown, which is critical and must be timed to the second because listeners and viewers will notice if there is "dead air" (an awkward pause in programming).

A television newscast is either thirty or sixty minutes long, and a local radio newscast is usually five to ten minutes long. The time allotment must include commercials, weather, sports, greetings, and farewells, which leaves about seventeen minutes of news for the average thirty-minute local television newscast. National network newscasts do not contain weather and sports, so the normal time allotment for news is about twenty-two minutes.

The speed at which anchors read is a critical element in how newscasts meet their time allotment, and producers take this into consideration when they finalize the scripts. When an anchor narrates a story during a newscast that has previously been taped, it is called a "voice over." As the voice over tape begins to roll, the anchor must read for the allotted amount of seconds. If the reading is too slow, the anchor could drown out the beginning of what the reporter says. If the reading is too fast, there could be dead air between the anchor's voice and the reporter's.

While the anchors read the news, the producer is usually in the control room monitoring the newscast and making sure the timing stays on schedule. He or she may talk to anchors through their hidden earphones, saying things like "speed up," "slow down," or "you're looking at the wrong camera."

Because news can happen at any time, even the most precisely planned newscast can go awry. For example, if a story is ready to be aired and a late-breaking news tip is received by the newsroom, everything may have to shift to make room for that story. Still, it is the producer's responsibility to make sure it all comes together as a cohesive, well-orchestrated program that happens within the allotted time.

> Cumulative time is the sum total of everything that's going to be broadcast, from the news to the feature stories to the commercials—each segment has a certain amount of seconds allotted. No matter how carefully we planned the newscast, at the last minute we could find ourselves scrambling to add or subtract something because the timing wasn't exactly right. If a news program is supposed to last exactly 30 minutes and it comes in at 29 minutes, that's one minute of dead air time. If you've ever seen anchors just chatting away at the end of a newscast, it's likely that someone mistimed the newscast and they have time to kill. It's not an ideal situation, but it happens in television. Learning to get timing right is a real science.[55]

Television producers who are responsible for the late night or early morning news programs perform many of the same tasks as those who produce the evening news. However, their schedules might not be quite as hectic. Stories that are written and footage that is shot during the day can be freshened and reused, so later news programs do not have to be created entirely from scratch.

Producers Who Work in Radio

Many radio stations have producers whose tasks are similar to those Poplin describes for television. While radio producers' responsibilities vary based on the size of the market and the station's format, it is common for them to coordinate news and program production from start to finish. They determine what news is covered and which reporters will cover and write it, sometimes even reporting and writing it themselves. At smaller stations, producers may also anchor the news on the air. Radio producers may coordinate a station's music lineup, but this is generally the responsibility of other staff such as program directors.

At radio stations that feature local talk shows, producers are responsible for developing the shows by selecting a topic, finding guests to be interviewed, and writing scripts. At stations that feature lengthy news programs, such as two-hour time blocks, producers schedule the order of the newscast. In large markets radio producers may supervise a team of assistant producers and production staff.

Producers who work for National Public Radio are responsible for developing such well-known news programs as *All Things Considered*, *NPR Morning Edition*, and *NPR Weekend Edition*. Thomas Looker has worked as a writer, producer, and reporter for NPR news programs and documentaries, and his description of the process NPR producers go through is not unlike that of television producers. He explains, "Creating a news program for the radio is neither wholly a science nor wholly an art. It is, in essence, an act of the human imagination: separating fantasy from truth, judging what's significant and what's not, deciding what will hold a listener's attention and what will turn it off."[56]

NPR producers work different shifts based on which programs they are responsible for and what time the programs are aired. Like their television counterparts, NPR producers craft the various programs that are broadcast to the public. They gather information from a variety of sources, including the wire services, about events around the country and throughout the world. Based on the information they collect, they make decisions about what to include in each program and prepare a rundown. Producers responsible for *Morning Edition*, which is live on the air at 6:00 A.M. each weekday, are usually at work by midnight. They, like producers of other NPR programs, have a two-hour slot to fill, so their challenge is to find enough information to shape each program into an interesting compilation of news reports, interviews, and commentaries that are broadcast on the air by NPR anchors.

Never-Ending Challenges

The success of any news program, whether it is at the national or local level, rests on the shoulders of producers, so they are constantly under intense pressure to make the right decisions about their stations' programming. For instance, if a producer is faced with choosing between three major stories, he or she must make a decision which story to lead with. If two other stations in the same market run a different lead story, the producer may be questioned by executive management about the validity of his or her choices.

Producers also make decisions about how much "hard news," as opposed to feature and local interest stories, to include in each

A team of producers compiles information for an upcoming broadcast.

broadcast—too much hard news, and the station may receive complaints that they are focusing on only the bad things that are happening. Too many feature or local interest stories, and the programs may be criticized for being too "fluffy."

In addition, there is always the danger of broadcasting a story that is incorrect or incomplete, which makes the station or network look bad in the eyes of the public. Credibility is extremely important, and producers are responsible for maintaining this credibility through their day-to-day programming decisions. If a station's credibility goes down, its ratings will go down with it, and the producers—especially the executive producer—are often held responsible.

Producers work very hard but because their positions are not visible to the public, they receive little recognition for the success of their programs. Elizabeth Wilson, a Los Angeles producer, describes the stress and hectic pace of her job: "Sometimes I feel like a juggler! Even though I like what I do, it's hard to keep all the balls in the air every day. And if I drop one, I know there's someone waiting in the wings—or on my own staff—ready to take my job and try to do it better."[57]

One constant challenge producers face is the necessity of working with a diverse team of news professionals. Although producers are ultimately responsible for programming, they must deal with reporters, anchors, photojournalists, and even other producers—all of whom have their own distinct personalities as well as their own

One Horrific Day in a Producer's Life

This excerpt is from Valerie Hyman's article, "The Producers's Challenge" from The Producer Book *on the Ohio University Scripps School of Journalism website. George Gillis, who spent many years as a broadcast producer and says he "managed to retain a semblance of sanity after many years in the business," describes a particularly harrowing day.*

One enters the newsroom at the beginning of one's shift and finds the anxiety level begins at "50" on a scale of 1–100. It goes up from there throughout the day. Breaking news requiring helicopter coverage seems to occur when the only available photographer doesn't "do" helicopters. The battery packs for cameras are all either discharged or have battery memory of two minutes. The chief photographer is [ill]. . . . The news director came in with a bad back and has had to fire someone to relieve his pain. . . . The male anchor has spent two hours trying to prove the producer was incorrect in his spelling of the word "restaurateur." . . . The assignment editor is virtually deaf from the 18 radios he keeps at full blast tracking EMS, police and fire departments of thirty jurisdictions, the competition and his wife's cell phone. The computer system is down. The script for the show has more blanks in it than copy. The top three stories are being done by reporters stuck in a massive traffic jam and are feeding their scripts by radio. The tape line-up for the show is lost. The male anchor's earphone has fallen out. The traffic department changed all the spots in the show. Top-level executives of a major multi-national corporation which just bought the station are in the control room and you have mistimed the show by thirty seconds.

ideas about what news stories should be broadcast and in what order. If producers have enough authority, they will evaluate the different opinions and make final programming decisions as they see fit. However, some producers feel they have "all the responsibility but none of the authority." In other words, they may be held accountable when things go wrong even though their decisions can be supplanted by others on the team.

Who Is Right for This Job?

Because of the stress that is inherent in a producer's job, as well as the constant demands and fast-paced schedule, most successful producers are competitive people who thrive on challenges. They have no problem working under pressure, and some even work best when things are the most stressful.

Producers are high-energy people. They are organized and can think quickly and make decisions when deadlines are looming and all around them is chaos. They get along well when working in teams with other news staff members, but they can also work independently and are not afraid to make decisions on their own, even if those decisions are not always popular with others. They are good at managing details and solving problems. They are creative and imaginative, and they are excellent writers and editors. Good listeners, they excel at communicating.

Most people who seek a career in television or radio dream of being an anchor or on-air personality rather than a producer, mainly because the perceived glamour of a broadcasting job revolves around the chance to be seen on television or heard on the radio, not working behind the scenes. Most people can name a dozen famous local and national anchors but few know the names of any producers. However, being a producer can be a challenging, rewarding career that requires a great deal of talent as well as passion for the news and all that goes into creating a news program.

Becoming a Producer

For anyone interested in a broadcast production career, hands-on experience is by far the most important thing—more important, even, than a college degree. However, while it is true that some producers have gotten where they are in their careers solely because of their experience, the news media is very competitive. That means people who have a bachelor's degree have a far better chance of get-

Journalism students train to work in television production. College programs allow students to experience a careerlike setting.

ting hired for their first production jobs than those without a college education.

Young people interested in a production career would benefit from a college program that specializes in journalism or broadcast journalism because the curriculum so closely relates to the career. In addition, English and writing classes are essential because most producers research and write news stories. Studying forensics and drama helps develop poise and speaking skills as well as confidence. And classes in history, government, and political science are valuable because producers, like all news media professionals, need a good understanding of the world around them.

It is crucial that aspiring producers seek out as much on-the-job experience as possible. This could include job shadowing or volunteering to assist at a local television or radio station. Extracurricular activities, such as working on the production of high school plays or community theater performances, help students learn how to manage details and work with teams of people. Multiple internships during high school and college are essential because they not only provide hands-on training but also can lead to future employment opportunities. Juliet Dragos, who is now a television news anchor but spent many years as a television producer, says this about her college internship:

> I took TV classes in high school and I loved it. Then during my senior year of college, where I was majoring in broadcasting, I got an internship at an NBC affiliate in Pittsburgh, which is one of the major markets. In one semester at that station I learned more about TV than during three whole years of college. When I graduated, I was offered a job there. So the internship paid off for me—in more ways than one.[58]

When producers are hired for their first jobs they usually start out as production assistants, where they build their knowledge and gain experience in the technical and creative areas of radio or television production. At first they may find themselves somewhat dismayed because their jobs can include such mundane tasks as proofreading news copy and even coordinating staff meetings. But this is just part of being newcomers. Once they have proven themselves and gained enough experience, their next step is usually to producer positions.

Because of the fast-paced nature of broadcast news, producers may find the first few years to be a difficult learning period. Beginning producers typically end up working the shifts no one else wants to work, like the "graveyard" (late night) shift, and they often work longer than the average workweek. *The Princeton Review* confirms this: "Long hours of grunt work tests a person's tenacity. . . . Work shifts can be 16 hours or more, and when an emergency arises, PAs [production assistants] are expected to stay and cope until it is resolved."[59]

Although it is true that the first few years can be a tough period of learning and development, it can result in valuable knowledge and training for aspiring producers. By learning the broadcast news business from beginning to end, they become more valuable to their employers and are likely to become promoted or find more prestigious production jobs in bigger markets.

Earnings and the Future

Salaries for producers vary widely based on the size of the market as well as years of experience. In general, television producers earn more money than those involved in radio. According to a salary survey by the Radio-Television News Directors Association, in 2000 the average salary for a television news producer was about $29,000, while the average salary for a radio producer was $27,300. In the largest markets television producers averaged about $50,000, while radio producers in those markets averaged $33,000. Of course, as producers gain experience and credibility with management, their salary potential can significantly increase. The survey showed that executive producers in television make annual salaries of well over $100,000 in major markets. Those who work in the largest markets and at national networks can earn significantly more.

All indications are that the future is bright for those who want to become producers, as the best opportunities for anyone entering broadcast news are in producing. Most young people who are interested in radio and television aspire to be on the air as television reporters or anchors or radio announcers, so producers are always in high demand. In fact, many students do not even consider production as a career. What many people are not aware of, however, is

Producers monitor a control panel in a television studio. The best opportunities for people entering television broadcasting are in production.

how much talent and creativity it takes to be a producer, and how essential this person is to a television or radio station. They also do not understand what a producer's job is actually like or how enjoyable it can be in spite of the challenges, as Cincinnati producer Robin Radin explains:

> One thing I really would have liked to learn in college is that there is a lot more to a newsroom than reporting and anchoring. Everyone I knew in the broadcast news program with me wanted to be on the air. We thought that was where all the control, power, creativity, and journalistic ability would be used. It was not until my first job outside of college that I learned that reporters, while having some flexibility for creativity and journalistic ability, really are under the mercy of management and the producers. It was there that I learned how much creativity the producers get to utilize, and how much writing the producers do. It was there that I realized I never, ever wanted to report, and that all I really wanted to do was produce.[60]

Chapter 5

Radio Announcers

Whether they are called announcers or on-air personalities, broadcasters or program hosts, the people whose voices are heard on the radio are crucial to the success of a radio station. After all, radio announcers are the station's only "product." They entertain people during talk shows and keep them informed about current news. They tell about traffic problems and alert listeners about current weather conditions. On music format stations, announcers play their listeners' favorite music. The fact is, many announcers become so familiar that people tune in faithfully, day after day. And popularity with their listening audience is extremely important to radio announcers. If people enjoy hearing them, they will keep tuning in. Otherwise, they will stop listening to them and tune to a different station. Dallas on-air personality Hollywood Henderson explains the relationship between a radio station and its listeners:

> What is a "listener payoff?" From a personality jock's viewpoint, it's saying something relevant, interesting, entertaining, memorable or engaging. (That's not an all-inclusive list!) It's like scoring a point in tennis, or hitting the target with another arrow. From the listener's viewpoint, it's a feeling of satisfaction, of having needs met, of "completeness" they get from listening to your station. Or SHOULD get, or they won't hang around very long![61]

Relying on Radio for the News

While some listeners tune in to their favorite radio stations primarily to hear talk shows and music, radio is an important source of news for many people. They may choose television for evening news broadcasts when they are at home, but when they are driving, working, or playing, radio has been shown to be people's number-one choice for hearing the news. Stations that have a combination music and news format often broadcast five-minute news segments only at the "top of the hour," which means at noon, 1:00 P.M., 2:00 P.M., etc., and sometimes on the half hour as well. Stations that have all news or combination news/talk radio formats broadcast the news throughout the day, and many of these stations feature programming from National Public Radio (NPR).

Every week approximately 10 million people listen to NPR news and commentary programs that are broadcast at nearly five hundred radio stations all over the country. The announcers who host these programs on the air are as famous as any well-known television anchors, and are highly respected by other media professionals. Bob Edwards is one of them. He hosts NPR's *Morning Edition*, the most popular program in public radio, and he has held this position since the show premiered in 1979. When asked what makes radio special as a way of delivering the news, Edwards had this to say:

> It's . . . a more personal medium. It seems to go directly to one's brain. There are no pictures to distract. The pictures are created by the listener, with a little help from the broadcaster. The pictures are perfect. If you're showing pictures, different things in that picture can distract from the spoken word. So maybe the viewer is not absorbing everything the viewer should absorb. The viewer is looking at the correspondent instead of listening, thinking "oh, she's done something with her hair." Or "doesn't she look lovely in red?" With radio, the listener absorbs everything. In my case, the listener is often in an automobile driving to work. You can concentrate on the road while still getting an audio message that can be riveting.[62]

Types of Radio Announcers

The types of announcers who work at a radio station vary based on the size of the station and its particular format. Some different formats include all news; combination music and news; and news and talk radio, which often features "nationally syndicated" talk shows. *The Howard Stern Show, Dr. Laura,* and *Rush Limbaugh* are all examples of syndicated programs—programs recorded, produced,

Do People Still Listen to the Radio?

Despite the fact that television is the most popular medium for news and entertainment, the radio is still the most common wireless communication device on earth. Because of their portability, radios are everywhere from cars to homes, from offices to portable boom boxes found on the beach. Plus, 20 percent of Americans are now listening to their favorite radio stations online. According to a 1998 survey by Arbitron, at least 95 percent of teenagers and adults listen to the radio each week, and they tune in for an average of twenty-two hours per week. What all this means for radio announcers is that there will continue to be job opportunities for them.

Currently there are almost thirteen thousand radio stations broadcasting across the country. They have many different "formats," which means the types of music and/or news programs they offer, such as Top 40, Urban, Adult Contemporary, Country, and News/Talk. Most people typically listen to the radio when they get up in the morning and during the day while they commute to work or school, as well as at their workplace. During the weekend people tend to listen between 9:00 A.M. and 3:00 P.M.

In a report entitled *The American Radio News Audience Survey*, the Radio-Television News Directors Association found that 58 percent of the people who listen to the radio select their favorite stations based on the music that is played, and 21 percent choose stations because of news. Other reasons for choosing radio stations include entertainment, radio personalities, and weather/traffic/sports.

A radio announcer tapes a music program.

and then sold to stations all over the country who broadcast them along with their own local programming.

At larger stations there are often a number of announcers and jobs that are specialized; in other words, news, sports, and weather and traffic reports may each be assigned to one or more different announcers. At smaller stations a few people typically handle all these responsibilities.

General announcers, who are often called on-air personalities, are the hosts of particular radio programs. At a station that has a music format, one of their primary tasks is to introduce the music they play. They also introduce commercials that have been prerecorded, and sometimes they interview guests live on the air. They typically spend some of their airtime chatting about subjects they think might interest their listeners, and they invite listeners to call into the station and express their thoughts and opinions. And while they may not necessarily specialize in news, many announcers write news scripts and read the news as part of their regular programs.

Another type of radio announcer is a newscaster, who specializes in broadcasting news programs. Frequently referred to as news anchors, these people have the responsibility to create news broadcasts that include local, national, and world news. Newscasters collect information from the wire services (like the Associated Press and United Press International) and local sources, and decide which news should be included in each broadcast. Radio newscasters also may have reporter responsibilities and do their own interviewing and writing as well as broadcast the news on the air.

Sportscasters collect information on local and national sports and prepare sports reports to be broadcast. They handle live play-by-play coverage at area sporting events for high school, college, and local professional teams. They may also conduct interviews with sports personalities to be taped for later broadcasts. Dan Rusanowsky, the play-by-play radio announcer for the San Jose Sharks professional hockey team, says he loves his job because it allows him to combine his love of hockey with creativity. He explains, "It really is an art to do what I do. Hockey is a very dramatic sport. I love the challenge of painting a picture on the radio for the listener."[63]

Unlike at large radio stations where announcers are more specialized, at small stations it is common for them to perform a wide variety of tasks. They may play music and interview guests on the air

A radio announcer introduces a record while adjusting the soundboard. Announcers perform a variety of tasks.

or tape interviews for later broadcast. They sometimes perform engineering duties such as operating the soundboard, which is a device that controls all the station's audio. They often perform reporter duties, researching and writing news stories and broadcasting the news on the air. They may select and write the sports news and announce weather and traffic reports. They may have responsibility for writing and producing commercials as well as introducing them, and they even may be asked to sell commercial time to the station's advertisers. In general, the smaller the station, the more varied the announcers' tasks.

A Day with a News Announcer

Radio announcers' hours vary based on the time of the day they are on the air, and their tasks vary based on the size of the station and their specialty. Ken Robinson spent nineteen years as news announcer for WGAR, a major market (large) station in Cleveland, Ohio. He says while all stations are different, these tasks are typical for someone in his profession.

From the time Robinson arrived at the station at 10:30 A.M., his schedule was packed. He began his day by meeting with the morning crew to discuss stories that needed to be followed up for the day's news stories. He then checked the wire services and contacted local law enforcement authorities for any late-breaking local news. He monitored competitive radio stations to see what they were working on and reviewed local newspapers as well as faxes that came into the station from local officials.

Throughout the day Robinson worked on interviews and stories for his *News at Noon* program and his late afternoon and early evening broadcasts. He continued monitoring the wire services and competitive radio and television stations, and he wrote news stories that he broadcast on the air. He also developed and wrote a weekend public affairs show as well as various daily public affairs features.

Robinson says that while these are typical daily activities for a news announcer, there is always the possibility that something can happen to radically change the schedule. He explains: "Any day can be interrupted by the need for crisis coverage, assorted news and sports bulletins, plus phone calls from listeners, public relations people, news tipsters, visits from news makers, meetings with staff and management, special events coverage, extra paperwork, computer breakdowns, station tours, etc."[64]

The Pros and Cons of a Radio Career

One only has to listen to a local radio show to figure out that radio announcers have a good time doing what they do. The atmosphere is usually fun and relaxed, and everyone is part of the camaraderie. At a station with a music format, announcers often have access to some of the best seats in the house for music concerts and other events. Sportscasters have opportunities to meet and interview famous sports figures and receive tickets to many kinds of sporting events. On a local level radio announcers are frequently treated as celebrities and asked to be masters of ceremonies (MCs) at concerts and festivals.

Unless they are out doing "remotes," which are live broadcasts in locations away from the station, radio announcers work in broadcast booths inside a radio station. Although the booths are generally small, they are quiet because of cushion-like soundproofing, and the work environment is pleasant. Also, the dress code in a radio station is relaxed—announcers and other employees usually can wear casual clothes like jeans to work. Even at a prestigious national network like NPR the atmosphere is casual, as Edwards explains: "You can get old, fat, bald and nobody knows and nobody cares. . . . Nobody cares about your wardrobe, what your tie looks like, or even if you're wearing one, and I don't."[65]

However, like any career, working in radio has its downside. Announcers may find themselves working on a show with people they may not like very much, but they still have to pretend to get along for the benefit of the listening audience. They are under pressure to stick to tight schedules because they have to follow the program director's rundown. Everything that is on the air—music, commercials, newscasts, taped interviews, weather, and traffic reports—has to be broadcast at precisely the right times throughout the day and night.

Another downside to a radio career is the unusual schedules; in fact, one of the first things announcers say when asked what is most challenging about a career in radio is "strange hours." Most stations broadcast twenty-four hours a day and announcers are needed for each of the on-air time slots, which are usually four hours long. Announcers scheduled to be on the air from 6:00 to 10:00 A.M. are often at the station by 5:00 A.M., or even earlier, to prepare for their broadcast. But after their time on the air is over, their workday is far

A radio interview with actor Michael Palin (right). The atmosphere at radio stations is often fun and relaxed.

from finished. Announcers attend meetings with other station staff members. They often record commercials and tape programs that will be aired later, and they also spend time doing remotes and making appearances at community events on behalf of their stations. Some days that start very early can stretch long into the night, and it can be exhausting.

Even some announcers who have risen through the ranks to become famous have to cope with schedules that are unusual. One example is Edwards, who has a schedule that is anything but normal. When most people are asleep, he is awake. And when most people are awake, he is asleep. He explains:

> I wake up at about 1 A.M. I'm in the office by 2 A.M. We're on the air at 5. Between 2 and 5 I'm reading to find out what's been going on while I've been asleep. I have to write the open—the introduction to each hour, and what we call "the return," which is the kicker at the bottom of each hour. I'll do interviews with people on the other side of the world, where they're making news. Some are pre-taped interviews because maybe we can't get that person live or maybe we're not sure it's going to work out right so we tape it an hour in advance. . . . That's what I'm doing up until 5 A.M. After each program

Some radio announcers work long hours.

> I'm fixing it, because we're on in other time zones, and when the news changes, I have to update it. I go home by noon, and I'm in bed by 6 p.m. I get up at 1 and do it again.[66]

Working unusual hours can take its toll on radio announcers' personal lives. Obviously if they have to be at work by 3:00 or 4:00 A.M. (or even earlier) they cannot stay out late at night, and they are usually limited to socializing with people who work the same hours. This can make announcers feel isolated from their friends and family. Also, the very nature of their work can make them feel lonely because unless they are teamed up with other announcers, they may spend their entire on-air shift alone in the broadcast booth.

How a Radio Career Starts

Many people are aware of the pitfalls of working in radio, yet they still dream of a radio career. In fact, there are some people who know from the time they are very young that they want to work in radio. They hear their favorite announcers on the air every day and see them making appearances around town, and they think "That will be me someday." They tape-record their own "radio shows" by interviewing family and friends and try to imitate the radio personalities they admire. Such was the case with Daria Albinger, who works as a news anchor at all-news radio station WINS in New York City. She explains:

> You know how some kids play cops or fireman when they're growing up? I played reporter . . . using a hairbrush or a wooden spoon for a microphone, while I copied the people I'd watch on the news. My favorite thing, though, was to pretend to do a radio newscast. My first one . . . [was] at age 11, as a fifth grader in a mock broadcast at Christie Elementary School in Plano, Texas. Little did my teachers know, they created a monster![67]

Edwards is another announcer who, when he was very young, dreamed of someday being in radio. He describes how his interest first began:

> I loved the radio. The radio was my pal. I was just crazy about it. I wanted to be one of the voices in the box. It was just a magical thing. These voices came out of the box, as well as

> music and news and drama. . . . I got to know every format of every station and who was on and what time. In the evening you could get these Clear Channel stations from all over the country. And I would wonder about these towns. I was encouraged to read aloud in class and vocalize. So that directs a person into "well, I'll make use of my voice." . . . [When I was] in college, I got interested in news because the world was coming apart. The civil rights movement, the antiwar movement, the women's rights movement. That focused my radio ambitions toward news.[68]

Anyone interested in breaking into the radio field needs to understand the qualities it takes to succeed in this career. Superb communication skills are essential—radio announcers must have an excellent command of English and be able to speak articulately and listen well. Courses in public speaking and drama can help with this, as can acting in school and community theater productions or participating on school debate teams. Since they may have to discuss a variety of subjects on the air, announcers need to be intelligent and well versed on what is going on in the world around them.

Aspiring radio announcers with a four-year college degree in broadcast journalism or communications will definitely benefit from what they learn in school, and they may have an edge over those without a college degree—but this is not always the case. Most station managers emphasize qualities like communication skills, voice quality, and a pleasing personality. They pay particular attention to the sound of a person's voice, vocabulary, and way of enunciating. This is where practice makes perfect: By listening to their favorite radio and television personalities and paying attention to how they speak, aspiring radio announcers can dramatically improve their own speaking skills. Practicing with a tape recorder can also help because people often sound very different to themselves than they do to others.

A crucial quality for radio announcers is sounding natural on the air so the audience feels comfortable listening to them. One way to achieve this is to imagine they are talking personally to each listener, rather than talking to an audience of thousands. Dave Cruse, host of *The Morning Cruse* at WJIS/WLPJ in Sarasota/Tampa Bay, Florida, explains:

A Radio Show That Terrified

Years ago radio was much more than just a source of music and news; it was also a primary source of entertainment. Millions of Americans tuned in daily to hear their favorite radio programs like *Little Orphan Annie*, *The Lone Ranger*, *The Guiding Light*, and *The Shadow*.

A show that was broadcast on October 30, 1938, is one that stands out in radio history. Listeners, especially those in the eastern United States, experienced mass hysteria in response to a broadcast by a well-known radio actor named Orson Welles. The program was called "War of the Worlds," and it convinced thousands of people that an interplanetary conflict had started, and that Martians were spreading death and destruction in New Jersey and New York.

The radio play was created to simulate a regular radio program with a "break-in" for the material of the play. Listeners apparently did not hear the introduction, which said: "The Columbia Broadcasting System and its affiliated stations present Orson Welles and the Mercury Theatre on the Air in 'The War of the Worlds' by H.G. Wells." They also did not hear three additional announcements about the fictional nature of the program; thus, because the show was so realistic, it created widespread panic.

The broadcast disrupted households and created traffic jams as terrified people fled their homes and prepared to evacuate their cities. Thousands of people called the police, newspapers, and radio stations to seek advice on protective measures against the attacks, and many required medical treatment for shock and hysteria. Rumors about the Martian invasion spread quickly throughout the entire United States, and *The New York Times* reported some of these: Listeners in the Southeast heard that a planet "had struck in New Jersey with monsters . . . anywhere from 40 to 7,000 people [were] reported killed." In Indianapolis a woman reportedly ran into a church screaming: "New York is destroyed; it's the end of the world. You might as well go home to die. I just heard it on the radio." And in some cities, people told police and newspapers that they had actually seen the invasion for themselves.

As a result of the nationwide panic over the "War of the Worlds" broadcast, the Columbia Broadcasting System issued a statement expressing its regrets and announced that it would never again use the technique of a simulated news broadcast in its programming.

> The best way to endear yourself to your audience is to "be real." If you're funny, be funny. If you're warm and fuzzy, be warm and fuzzy. But don't try to be something you're not. . . . You don't have to sound like a radio announcer and you don't have to spit out one-liners like an Uzi with a jammed trigger. Forced humor isn't funny. Just share your life with people. Talk about your family, your kids, your trip to the beach or last week's sermon. Treat the audience like a friend. . . . Picture one person and speak to [him or her].[69]

One way for someone to get started in radio is to volunteer at a local station to get hands-on experience. Many communities have listener-sponsored radio stations that are funded solely by listeners and sponsoring corporations. Because they are commercial-free and receive no advertising revenue, these stations have small budgets and frequently use volunteers to operate radio equipment and even work as announcers. Jeff Kosloski, an advertising professional who now lives in Denver, spent two years as a part-time announcer at WYCE, a listener-sponsored radio station in Grand Rapids, Michigan. WYCE uses volunteers as announcers, and Kosloski says volunteering is an excellent way for someone interested in radio to break into the field because of everything they can learn on the job. He explains:

> At big radio stations there are different people to handle the work. All the announcers have to do is sit in the broadcast booth with headphones on and talk into the microphone. An engineer runs the soundboard. Then there's a program director who decides what music gets played and when, and people to write the news and commercials. Not so with a station like WYCE. There were times when I was the only person there and I did everything—chose the music, played the music, announced the music, and ran the board. I also wrote and read promos for our sponsors, talked to listeners on the phone, read news clips from wire services, and did the sports, weather, and traffic updates. Basically I made up my program as I went along, and that was one of the coolest things about working for a listener-sponsored station. Every show was uniquely me. And I learned a lot from the experience.[70]

Earnings and Opportunities

Radio is a career that can be extremely lucrative—but it does not start out that way. In 1998 half of all the announcers in the United States earned from just under $13,000 per year to about $28,000 per year, with those who specialized in news, sports, or weather generally earning more than general announcers. The smaller markets offer much lower salaries than larger markets, but these are the places where beginning announcers are more likely to find their first jobs. Over time, announcers build their knowledge and experience and move on to larger markets where the pay is better. In fact, it is common for announcers to relocate to different cities several times throughout their careers.

There is a huge variance in salaries paid to radio announcers around the country. In Buffalo, New York, for example, salaries range from $15,000 to $200,000 per year. Experienced announcers in large markets, especially those who do popular morning shows, can earn six-figure salaries. In major markets like New York some even earn millions, but it takes years of experience and a proven track record (as well as immense popularity) in order to get to that point.

A radio personality cues a record for play. Although working in radio can be lucrative, competition can be fierce for entry-level applicants.

Because there are nearly thirteen thousand radio stations broadcasting in the United States alone, there are opportunities for newcomers to break into the radio field. However, competition can be fierce as there are many young people who want radio careers. In fact, studies show that there are three times more entry-level applicants than there are jobs available. At national networks like NPR, the requirements are greater than at local stations (a college degree is a must) and the competition is extremely heavy.

Today Edwards is a well-known NPR announcer, but his career started at a tiny radio station in New Albany, Indiana, across the river from Louisville, Kentucky, where he grew up. He describes what the early days were like: "It was like working at a little paper where you learned to set type, sell ads, do obituaries, cover fires. That's what working at a small radio station is like. You have to spin records, fix the plumbing, try to sell ads. It's a good place to learn. The audience is small so you can be bad."[71] Today, after being at his job for over twenty years, Edwards's enthusiasm for his job at NPR is every bit as strong as it was when he started. He explains, "I'm still excited at being at a microphone and talking to listeners. I love that. It's the most basic element of what I do and I still enjoy it very much."[72]

Notes

Introduction: Keeping the Public Informed

1. Carl Filoreto and Lynn Setzer, *Working in T.V. News*. Memphis: Mustang Publishing, 1993, pp. 136–37.
2. Seth Mydans, "Ask a Reporter," Student Connections, New York Times On the Web. www.nytimes.com/learning/students/ask_reporters/mydans.html.

Chapter One: Reporters

3. Mydans, "Ask a Reporter."
4. Vernon Stone, "TV and Radio News Careers: Pros and Cons," Television and Radio Research News. www.missouri.edu/~jourvs/careerww.html.
5. Ted White, *Broadcast News Writing, Reporting, and Producing*. Newton, MA: Focal Press/Butterworth-Heinemann, 1996, p. 157.
6. Quoted in White, *Broadcast News Writing, Reporting, and Producing*, p. 167.
7. Keith Bradsher, "Ask a Reporter," Student Connections, New York Times On the Web. www.nytimes.com/learning/students/ask_reporters/bradsher.html.
8. Joe Grimm, "There's a Place for You," Jobs Page, *Detroit Free Press*. www.freep.com/jobspage/high/jrhigh.htm.
9. Tamar Lewin, "Ask a Reporter," Student Connections, New York Times On the Web. www.nytimes.com/learning/students/ask_reporters/ lewin.html.
10. Filoreto and Setzer, *Working in T.V. News*, pp. 61–62.
11. Filoreto and Setzer, *Working in T.V. News*, p. 40.
12. Quoted in "Working on Dangerous Assignments," European Journalism Centre. www.ejc.nl/hp/da/dahidden.html.
13. Bradsher, "Ask a Reporter."
14. Quoted in Vernon Stone, "Internships in TV and Radio News: Paid and Unpaid," Television and Radio News Research. www.missouri.edu/~jourvs/ginterns.html.

15. Quoted in Melanie D. Goldman, "Up Close and Personal," *Next Step Magazine*. www.nextstepmagazine.com/Career_Exploration/?article=up_close.

16. Filoreto and Setzer, *Working in T.V. News*, pp. 77–78.

17. Mydans, "Ask a Reporter."

Chapter Two: Photojournalists

18. "Pulitzer Prize Photographer: Carol Guzy," Live Online, *Washington Post*, April 21, 2000. http://discuss.washingtonpost.com/wp-srv/zforum/ 00/photo_guzy0421.htm.

19. Nancy L. Ford, "Photojournalism from the Soul," Photos@NL-Ford.com. www.nlford.com.

20. Mark Hertzberg, "Behind the Viewfinder: A Year in the Life of Photojournalism," Digital Storyteller. www.digitalstoryteller.com/BTV00/hertzberg/000418.shtml.

21. Filoreto and Setzer, *Working in T.V. News*, p. 41.

22. Quoted in, "Pulitzer Prize Photographer: Carol Guzy."

23. Bruce Conover, "Caught in the Crossfire," *IPI Report*, No. 1, 2001, International Press Institute. www.freemedia. at/IPIReport 1.01/ipirep1.01_7.htm.

24. Quoted in Fabi and Associates, "Biography of Warren Faidley, Storm Chasing Photographer," Cyclonecowboy.com. www.cyclonecowboy.com.

25. Quoted in Fabi and Associates, "Biography of Warren Faidley."

26. Filoreto and Setzer, *Working in T.V. News*, p. 41.

27. Michael D. Sherer, "Excellence in Television Photojournalism," Making the Commitment: Achieving Excellence in Television Photojournalism, National Press Photographers Association. www.ibiblio.org/nppa/sherer/sherer05.html.

28. Quoted in Bradley Wilson, "Careers in Photojournalism—A Chance to Document History," National Press Photographers Association. www.nppa.org/services/pjedu/careers.html.

29. Quoted in Trish Barker, "Advice: Shoot, Shoot, Shoot," *Spike Magazine*, University of Illinois College of Communications. www.comm.uiuc.edu/spike/mazzenga/advice.html.

30. Quoted in "On the Spot, Media & Communications," Get That Gig.com. www.gethatgig.com/media/careers/c_phjourn_suntimes.html.

31. Nancy L. Ford, "Photojournalism as a Career," Photos@NL Ford.com. www.nlford.com.
32. Carol Guzy, "Capturing a soul is worth 1,000 words," IPI Report, no. 2, 2001, International Press Institute. www.freemedia.at/IPI Report2.01/ipigj2.01_6.htm.

Chapter Three: Television Anchors

33. Robert Goldberg and Gerald Jay Goldberg, *Anchors: Brokaw, Jennings, Rather and the Evening News*. New York: Birch Lane Press/Carol Publishing, 1990, p. 9.
34. "John McQuiston: On Air Performance," John McQuiston's website. www.angelfire.com/biz/tvq/perform.html.
35. Juliet Dragos, WZZM-TV, Grand Rapids, Michigan, interview with author, November 15, 2001.
36. Quoted in Jennifer Orlando, "A glamorous job? 'NOT SO!' says Terri O," Puma Press section of Paradise Valley Community College. www.pvc.maricopa.edu/puma/apr00/lynx2.html.
37. Quoted in Judith Marlane, *Women in Television News Revisited*. Austin: University of Texas Press, 1999, p. 52.
38. Quoted in "Cronkite reports the death of President Kennedy," Rundown. www.tvrundown.com/lostdcro.htm.
39. Dragos, interview with author.
40. Quoted in "Reporting Live," "Media & Communications," Get That Gig. www.getthatgig.com/media/careers/c_anchor_fox.html.
41. Quoted in Chris Betros, "In Person: Wake-up call," Metropolis *Japan Today*. www.tokyoclassified.com/tokyointerview/390/tokyo interviewinc.htm.
42. Dragos, interview with author.
43. Dragos, interview with author.
44. Quoted in Orlando, "A glamorous job? 'NOT SO!' says Terri O."
45. Quoted in Orlando, "A glamorous job? 'NOT SO!' says Terri O."
46. Quoted in Marlane, *Women in Television News Revisited*, p. 210.
47. "Announcers," U.S. Department of Labor, *Occupational Outlook Handbook*, 2002–2003. www.bls.gov/oco/ocos087.htm.
48. Dragos, interview with author.
49. Quoted in Marlane, *Women in Television News Revisited*, p. 219.

Chapter Four: Broadcast Producers

50. Valerie Hyman, "The Producer's Challenge," *The Producer Book*, Ohio University Scripps School of Journalism. www.scripps.ohiou.edu/producer/thebook/chapter1.htm#challenge.

51. Quoted in Alice Main, "The Boss's Job: Do You Want It?" *The Producer Book*, Ohio University Scripps School of Journalism. www.scripps.ohiou.edu/producer/thebook/chapter5.htm.

52. Al Tompkins, "What News Directors Want from Producers," Doing Journalism, Poynter Institute. www.poynter.org/dj/tips/broadcast/directors.htm.

53. Ed Poplin, interview with author, November 25, 2001.

54. White, *Broadcast News Writing, Reporting, and Producing*, p. 155.

55. Poplin, interview with author.

56. Thomas Looker, *The Sound and the Story: NPR and the Art of Radio*. New York: Houghton Mifflin, 1995.

57. Quoted in "Producer—a Day in the Life," Career Center, Hobson's College View. www.collegeview.com/career/careersearch/ job_profiles/mc/pro02.html.

58. Dragos, interview with author.

59. "Television Producer," Career Profile, *Princeton Review*. www.review.com/career/careerProfile.cfm?id=156.

60. Robin Radin, "What Students Need to Know (or, What I Wish I Learned)," *The Producer Book*, Ohio University Scripps School of Journalism. www.scripps.ohiou.edu/producer/thebook/chapter3.htm.

Chapter Five: Radio Announcers

61. Hollywood Henderson, "Five Elements of a Great Show," Jocks Lounge, Relentless Radio. www.relentlessradio.com/jocks/ 05-00-Henderson-5elements.htm.

62. Quoted in "Interview with NPR's Bob Edwards—October 2000," *JournalismJobs* website. www.journalismjobs.com/interview_bobedwards.cfm.

63. Quoted in Rebecca Ray, "Shark Watch," Los Gatos, California, *Weekly Times*, March 21, 2001. www.metroactive.com/papers/los.gatos.weekly-times/03.21.01/cover-0112.html.

64. Ken Robinson, "A Day in the Newsroom with Northeast Ohio Broadcaster Ken Robinson." www.kenrobinson.com/day.html.

65. Quoted in "Interview with NPR's Bob Edwards."
66. Quoted in "Interview with NPR's Bob Edwards."
67. Daria Albinger interview, Meet our Staff, 1010-WINS. http://1010wins.com/bios/BioFolder/bio_160100135/index_html.
68. Quoted in "Interview with NPR's Bob Edwards."
69. Dave Cruse, "Back to the Basics," Morning Show, Relentless Radio. www.relentlessradio.com/morningshow/01-00.htm.
70. Jeff Kosloski, interview with author, November 27, 2001.
71. Quoted in "Interview with NPR's Bob Edwards."
72. Quoted in "Interview with NPR's Bob Edwards."

Organizations to Contact

American Society of Newspaper Editors (ASNE)
11690B Sunrise Valley Dr.
Reston, VA 20191-1409
(703) 453-1122
website: www.asne.org

ASNE's purpose is to serve as a medium for exchange of ideas and the professional growth and development of its members (newspaper editors in the United States and Canada). It also seeks to improve the diversity, readership, and credibility of newspapers.

Broadcast Education Association (BEA)
1771 N St. NW
Washington, DC 20036-2891
(202) 429-5354
website: www.beaweb.org

BEA is dedicated to helping prepare college students to enter careers in radio and television as well as telecommunications and electronic media. Over thirteen hundred professors, students, and media professionals are currently individual members of the BEA, and approximately 250 college and university departments and schools are institutional members.

Investigative Reporters and Editors, Inc. (IRE)
Missouri School of Journalism
138 Neff Annex
Columbia, MO 65211
(573) 882-2042
website: www.ire.org

IRE is a grassroots nonprofit organization dedicated to improving the quality of investigative reporting within the field of journalism. The organization was formed to create a networking tool and a forum in which journalists from across the country could raise questions and exchange ideas.

National Scholastic Press Association (NSPA)
2221 University Ave. SE, Suite 121
Minneapolis, MN 55414
(612) 625-8335
website: www.studentpress.org

NSPA is dedicated to helping high school students become better reporters, writers, editors, photographers, designers, desktop publishers, and advertising and business staffers.

The Poynter Institute
801 Third St. South
St. Petersburg, FL 33701
(727) 821-9494
website: www.poynter.org

The Poynter Institute is a school for journalists, future journalists, and teachers of journalism. The organization's mission is to teach and inspire journalists and media leaders.

Radio-Television News Directors Association (RTNDA)
1600 K St. NW, Suite 700
Washington, DC 20006-2838
(202) 659-6510
website: www.rtndf.org

RTNDA is the world's largest and only professional organization exclusively serving the electronic news profession. It is made up of more than three thousand news directors, news associates, educators, and students, and its purpose is to set standards of excellence in news gathering and reporting.

Youth Radio
1809 University Ave.
Berkeley, CA 94703
(510) 841-5123
website: www.youthradio.org
Youth Radio promotes young people's intellectual, creative, and professional growth through training and access to media. In a variety of ways, the organization helps students learn the basics of broadcasting and exposes them to a wide array of media-related careers.

For Further Reading

Jeff Alan, *Responsible Journalism: A Practical Guide for Working and Aspiring Journalists*. Chicago: Bonus Books, 2001. Explores the ethical difficulties facing journalists today using real-life examples to offer solutions to complicated problems facing anyone in the industry: public scrutiny, the pressure of deadlines, and the increasing push for ratings. More than a guide for journalism students, the book is also a study in how journalists think, behave, and misbehave.

Bob Arya, *Thirty Seconds to Air*. Ames: Iowa State Press, 1999. Covers the professional and personal issues, concerns, and difficulties that a live broadcast reporter must confront and conquer in order to be successful. A great resource for aspiring reporters.

Brian Horton, *Associated Press Guide to Photojournalism*. New York: McGraw Hill, 2000. An insider's guide to the exciting career of photojournalism. Emphasizes the creative process behind the photojournalist's art based on the author's experience as well as the experiences of other award-winning photojournalists.

Brad Kalbfeld, *The Associated Press Broadcast News Handbook*. New York: McGraw Hill, 2001. A helpful guide to writing and delivering the news on radio, television, and other broadcast media. The main focus is on the art of finding, researching, writing, editing, producing, and delivering authoritative, accurate, and exciting news stories. Provides a wealth of information on key technical aspects involved, such as how to handle a microphone and how many tape recorders to carry in the field.

Kenneth Kobre, *Photojournalism: The Professionals' Approach*. Boston: Focal Press, 2000. A guide to the many facets of photojournalism such as how to get the best shots when on assignment, covering spot or general news, or doing features or portraits. Also covers the history of photojournalism.

Deborah Copaken Kogan, *Shutterbabe: Adventures in Love and War*. New York: Villard Books, 2000. A story of the author's desire to be a photojournalist and her four-year journey to see and photograph the world. It tells of her personal and professional experiences as a photojournalist, covering everything from conflict in Haiti to the fall of communism in Romania—a violent contrast to her upbringing in suburban Maryland.

Jeff Leshay, *How to Launch Your Career in TV News*. Lincolnwood, IL: VGM Career Horizons, NTC Publishing Group, 1993. Television news is a highly competitive field and that first job is always the most difficult to acquire. Leshay uses descriptions from prominent individuals, and also much of his text, to advise the reader on the ins and outs of the job search and interview preparation.

Ken Lindner, *Broadcasting Realities: Real-Life Issues and Insights for Broadcast Journalists, Aspiring Journalists and Broadcasters*. Chicago: Bonus Books, 1999. Targeted at broadcasters and aspiring broadcasters, this book examines the ethical and practical decisions behind the scenes of broadcasting's biggest stories.

William Serrin, *The Business of Journalism: Ten Leading Reporters and Editors on the Pitfalls of the Press*. New York: New Press, 2000. Includes inspiring stories about journalists who have fought to uphold the ideals of their profession, even when it has been a battle.

Mitchell Stephens, *Broadcast News*. Fort Worth: Harcourt Brace Jovanovich, 1993. *The New York Times* rates this book the "most widely used introduction to radio and television journalism." It has been used, in its three editions, at hundreds of colleges and universities.

Dan Weaver and Jason Siegel, *Breaking into Television: Proven Advice from Veterans and Interns*. Princeton, NJ: Peterson's, 1998. Provides valuable insight into what a television career is really like through the eyes of seasoned TV veterans (all former interns) and network executives. A helpful guide for anyone interested in pursuing a career in the television field.

Steve Weinberg, *The Reporter's Handbook—An Investigator's Guide to Documents and Techniques*. New York: St. Martin's Press, 1996. A step-by-step guide on how to follow the paper trail, how to background an individual, and how to use computers in conducting research. Includes virtually everything an aspiring reporter needs to know about finding information.

Ray White, *TV News: Building a Career in Broadcast Journalism*. Boston: Focal Press, 1990. Explores the realities and opportunities for newcomers in the world of television news.

Works Consulted

Books

Elmo I. Ellis, *Opportunities in Broadcasting Careers*. Lincolnwood, IL: VGM Career Horizons, NTC Publishing Group, 1992. A reference guide for anyone considering a career in broadcasting. It includes an overview of the field, career preparation including educational requirements, descriptions of each segment of the broadcast media, and ways to advance in a broadcasting career.

Carl Filoreto and Lynn Setzer, *Working in T.V. News*. Memphis: Mustang Publishing, 1993. An honest, amusing, and informative guide to a career in television news. It includes in-depth descriptions of the life of a television journalist and includes details on the various jobs available, advice about what news directors look for when they consider applicants, and a listing of television stations in the United States and Canada.

Robert Goldberg and Gerald Jay Goldberg, *Anchors: Brokaw, Jennings, Rather and the Evening News*. New York: Birch Lane Press/Carol Publishing, 1990. Profiles of the careers of three of the most famous anchors in television history including a look at how the news is created at national networks.

Thomas Looker, *The Sound and the Story: NPR and the Art of Radio*. New York: Houghton Mifflin, 1995. A thoughtful and entertaining "inside look" at National Public Radio. It includes details about how the different shows are produced, perspectives from the behind-the-scenes professionals at NPR, and revealing looks at such famous NPR commentators as Bob Edwards, Susan Stamberg, and Linda Wertheimer.

Judith Marlane, *Women in Television News Revisited*. Austin: University of Texas Press, 1999. Includes the personal accounts of seventy prominent women in television news and their opinions on subjects such as how they achieved success, the pitfalls and triumphs of their careers, how it is different for women vs. men in the world of television, and the gains women have made in television journalism. It also includes perspectives from fifteen well-known male anchors.

Ted White, *Broadcast News Writing, Reporting, and Producing*. Newton, MA: Focal Press/Butterworth-Heinemann, 1996. A comprehensive book about broadcast news that covers the skills, techniques, and challenges of writing, reporting, and producing news for broadcast. It includes many real-life news examples along with scripts and interviews of well-known broadcast professionals who have covered the news stories.

Internet Sources

Daria Albinger interview, Meet Our Staff, 1010-WINS. http://1010wins.com/bios/BioFolder/bio_160100135/index_html. Announcer Daria Albinger discusses her early desire to be in radio and her career path to get where she is today.

"Announcers," U.S. Department of Labor, *Occupational Outlook Handbook*, 2002–2003. www.bls.gov/oco/ocos087.htm. This handbook includes such information as nature of the work, working conditions, employment and training, job outlook, and earnings.

Trish Barker, "Advice: Shoot, Shoot, Shoot," *Spike Magazine*, University of Illinois College of Communications. www. comm.uiuc.edu/spike/mazzenga/advice.html. An in-depth interview with photojournalism veteran Anthony "Val" Mazzenga, who discusses his background, changes in photojournalism, and offers advice for aspiring photojournalists.

Chris Betros, "In Person: Wake-up call," Metropolis, *Japan Today*. www.tokyoclassified.com/tokyointerview/390/tokyointerviewinc.htm. Co-anchor of a Japanese morning news show, Betros talks about her typical day, including when things do not go as planned.

Keith Bradsher, "Ask a Reporter," Student Connections, New York Times On the Web. www.nytimes.com/learning/students/ask_reporters/bradsher.html. Detroit bureau chief Keith Bradsher answers students questions about life as a reporter.

Adriana Cacciottolo, "Prints of Darkness," *Maltese Times, Weekender Supplement, October 7, 1995*. www.darrinzammitlupi. com/aboutme5.htm. The biography of a well-known photojournalist who shares his perspective on the art of press photography.

"Career Biographies—Television Photojournalist," interview with Steve Affens, Teen Division, Internet Public Library. www.ipl.org/teen/pathways/art-ent/tvphoto.html. A television photojournalist shares his views on the qualities one needs to succeed in this career, as well as the responsibility to the Constitution's declaration of freedom of the press.

Bruce Conover, "Caught in the Crossfire," *IPI Report*, No. 1, 2001, International Press Institute. www.freemedia.at/ IPIReport1.01/ipirep1.01_7.htm. A CNN producer relates his experience while on a dangerous assignment in the Middle East.

"Cronkite reports the death of President Kennedy," Rundown. www.tvrundown.com/lostdcro.htm. A veteran newsman's account of the difficulty of covering a national tragedy, and his views on what it takes to be a good journalist.

Dave Cruse, "Back to the Basics," Morning Show, Relentless Radio. www.relentlessradio.com/morningshow/01-00.htm. Advice for announcers on the basics of a good radio show, including how to "be real" when talking to listeners.

Jessica Dumpert, "Anchor of NBC Morning News Show Returns to COM for Visit," College of Communication, Boston University. www.bu.edu/com/alumni/source/Articles/Current_News/1998/May/NBC_Anchor/a_str_01.html. A morning news anchor discusses her experience in the television field.

Tim Engle, "We Interrupt This Program," *Kansas City Star*, April 25, 2001, Information Technology Careers, *Kansas City Star*. www.kcstar.com/item/pages/local.pat,fyi/3acc9f05.425,.html. Several television meteorologists discuss their job responsibilities and the equipment they use in forecasting the weather.

Fabi and Associates, "Biography of Warren Faidley, Storm Chasing Photographer," Cyclonecowboy.com. www.cyclonecowboy.com. An in-depth profile of a photojournalist who specializes in hurricanes, cyclones, and wildfires, and other natural disasters.

Ricky Flores, "Witness to Tragedy," Stories Amidst the Chaos. National Press Photographers Association. www.nppa.org/wtc/flores/default.htm. A photojournalist's personal account of his filming in New York after the World Trade Center terrorist attack on September 11, 2001.

Nancy L. Ford, "Photojournalism as a Career," Photos@NLFord.com. www.nlford.com. A discussion of a photojournalism career and the photojournalist's responsibility to capture reality and truth through the camera.

———, "Photojournalism from the Soul," Photos@NLFord.com. www.nlford.com. Ford's personal essay on the soul of photojournalism, and what makes a great photo.

Melanie D. Goldman, "Up Close and Personal," *Next Step Magazine*. www.nextstepmagazine.com/Career_ Exploration/ ?article=up_close. An interview with T.J. Winick, a busy television reporter who discusses how he got his job, what a typical day is like, and sacrifices he has made to get where he is today.

Joe Grimm, "There's a Place for You," Jobs Page, *Detroit Free Press*. www.freep.com/jobspage/high/jrhigh.htm. A *Detroit Free Press* recruiting and development director gives valuable insight into what newspaper professionals are like, and discusses what makes a good newspaper reporter or writer.

Carol Guzy, "Capturing a soul is worth 1,000 words," IPI Report, no. 2, 2001, International Press Institute. www.freemedia.at/ IPIReport2.01/ipigj2.01_6.htm. Guzy discusses the spirit of the photojournalist, and the privilege of recording both triumphs and tragedies.

Hollywood Henderson, "Five Elements of a Great Show," Jocks Lounge, Relentless Radio. www.relentlessradio.com/ jocks/05-00-Henderson 5elements.htm. Radio on-air personality Henderson offers his perspective on what makes the best radio show.

Mark Hertzberg, "Behind the Viewfinder: A Year in the Life of Photojournalism," Digital Storyteller. www.digitalstoryteller.com/ BTV00/hertzberg/000418.shtm. Photojournalist Mark Hertzberg discusses the joys and sadness captured by a camera.

Valerie Hyman, "The Producer's Challenge," *The Producer Book*, Ohio University Scripps Shool of Journalism. www.scripps.ohiou. edu/producer/thebook/chapter1.htm#challenge. Discusses the importance of photojournalists seeking out the truth and reporting it factually.

"Interview with NPR's Bob Edwards—October 2000," JournalismJobs. www.journalismjobs.com/interview_bobedwards.cfm. America's most famous NPR anchor shares his insight about how he got started in radio, what his career is like, and a typical day at NPR.

Tamar Lewin, "Ask a Reporter," Student Connection, New York Times On the Web. www.nytimes.com/learning/students/ask_reporters/ lewin.html. *New York Times* national reporter Tamar Lewin answers students' questions about life as a reporter.

Alice Main, "The Boss's Job: Do You Want It?" *The Producer Book*, Ohio University Scripps School of Journalism. www.scripps.ohiou.edu/producer/thebook/chapter5.htm. Provides an in-depth look at the responsibilities and challenges faced by executive producers.

"John McQuiston: On Air Performance," John McQuiston's website. www.angelfire.com/biz/tvq/perform.html. An anchorman offers advice to aspiring television professionals about being calm and confident and acting natural, no matter what is going on in the newsroom.

"On the Spot, Media Communications," Get that Gig.com. www. get thatgig.com/media/careers/c_phjourn_suntimes.html. An interview with photojournalist Jean Lachat, who describes her career as "a dream" and discusses such things as her career path and what a typical day is like.

Seth Mydans, "Ask a Reporter," Student Connections, New York Times On the Web. www.nytimes.com/learning/students/ask_reporters/mydans.html. Southeast Asia corresponsdent Seth Mydans answers students' questions about life as a reporter.

Jennifer Orlando, "A glamorous job? 'NOT SO!' says Terri O," Puma Press, Paradise Valley Community College. www.pvc.maricopa.edu/puma/apr00/lynx2.html. Well-known anchorwoman Terri Ouellette reveals the years of hard work it took her to get to where she is today and discusses the life of a news anchor.

"Photojournalism Timeline," Photojournalism Time Warner. http://tbssuperstation.com/d_sunday/dying/html/time_main.htm. Provides a brief synopsis of how the roots of photojournalism go back as far as the Civil War and how photojournalists today still risk their lives in their careers.

"Producer—a Day in the Life," Career Center, Hobson's College View. www.collegeview.com/career/careersearch/job_profiles/mc/pro02.html. Producer Elizabeth Wilson's candid depiction of the good points and bad points about her career.

"Pulitzer Prize Photographer: Carol Guzy," Live Online, *Washington Post*, April 21, 2000. http://discuss.washingtonpost.com/wp-srv/zforum/00/photo_guzy0421.htm. Three-time Pulitzer Prize winning photojournalist Carol Guzy answers questions about the life of a photojournalist.

Robin Radin, "What Students Need to Know (or, What I Wish I Learned)," The Producer Book, Ohio University's Scripps School of Journalism. www.scripts.ohiou.edu/producer/thebook/chapter3.htm. Discusses how colleges and universities should spend more time educating students about rewards of careers in broadcast producing.

"Radio's First Message," Institute of Electrical and Electronics Engineers. www.ewh.ieee.org/reg/7/millennium/radio/radio_home.html. Includes historical information about the first radio broadcast and Reginald Fessenden, the first voice ever to be heard on the radio.

Rebecca Ray, "Shark Watch," Los Gatos, California, *Weekly Times*, March 21, 2001. www.metroactive.com/papers/los.gatos.weekly-times/03.21.01/cover-0112.html. Pro team sports announcer Dan Rusanowsky discusses his career path to becoming a successful play-by-play sportscaster.

"Reporting Live," Media & Communications, Get That Gig. www.getthatgig.com/media/careers/c_anchor_fox.html. FOX-TV news anchor Toby Cook talks about a typical day in his career and includes some advice for aspiring television professionals.

Ken Robinson, "A Day in the Newsroom with Northeast Ohio Broadcaster Ken Robinson." www.kenrobinson.com/day.html. Robinson, a news announcer, gives a detailed description of what a typical day is like in his newsroom.

Michael D. Sherer, "Excellence in Television Photojournalism," Making the Commitment: Achieving Excellence in Television Photojournalism, National Press Photographers Association.

www.ibiblio.org/nppa/sherer/sherer05.html. A discussion about photojournalism ethics and expectations.

Vernon Stone, "Internships in TV and Radio News: Paid and Unpaid," Television and Radio News Research. www.missouri.edu/~jourvs/ginterns/html. Includes an in-depth look at how internships benefit aspiring broadcast news professionals.

———, "TV and Radio News Careers: Pros and Cons," Television and Radio News Research. www.missouri.edu/ujourvs/careerww.html. Covers many facets of a broadcast news career including advantages and challenges of the field, who makes a good broadcast news professional, and job availability.

Al Tompkins, "What News Directors Want from Producers," Doing Journalism, Poynter Institute. www.poynter.org/dj/tips/broad cast/directors.htm. Tompkins offers a news director's perspective on what makes producers successful.

Mike Wallace, "Why My Mind Has Changed About the Value of a National News Council," from a speech given at Harvard University, *Newsworthy*, Fall 1995, Minnesota Telecommunications Network. www.mtn.org/~newscncl/fall95/ Wallace.html. The famed *60 Minutes* host discusses the public's distrust and ill feelings toward the press.

Bradley Wilson, "Careers in Photojournalism—A Chance to Document History," National Press Photographers Association. www.nppa.org/services/pjedu/careers.html. A journalism executive discusses how photojournalism is a chance to capture history through the camera and how photojournalists must be prepared for anything.

"Working on Dangerous Assignments," European Journalism Centre. www.ejc.nl/hp/da/dahidden.html. An excellent description of the many dangers and hazards that reporters often face in their jobs.

Websites

Arbitron. (www.arbitron.com). This site includes demographical and statistical information about television and radio audiences.

The Pulitzer Prizes. www.pulitzer.org. An interesting collection of historical and factual information about the Pulitzer Prize including a list of frequently asked questions.

Radio-Television News Directors Association. www.rtndf.org. Includes research on radio and television audiences, broadcast news staffing, and salary information.

"Television Producer," Career Profile, *Princeton Review*. www.review.com/career/careerProfile.cfm?id=156. Provides a general overview of the life of a television producer.

Index

Picture Credits

© AFP/CORBIS, 13,19, 53
© Bettman /CORBIS, 28
© CORBIS, 46
© Ales Fevzer/CORBIS, 36
© Kevin Fleming/CORBIS, 67
© Owen Franken/CORBIS, 16
© Shelley Gazin/CORBIS, 77, 59
© Philip Gould/CORBIS, 73
Joshua S. Kotner, 75
© Robert Maass/CORBIS, 10
© Emmanuel Ortiz/CORBIS, 21
© Neal Preston/CORBIS, 25
© Roger Ressmeyer/CORBIS, 44, 57, 83
© Reuters NewMedia Inc./CORBIS, 31, 51, 64
© Bob Rowan; Progressive Image/CORBIS, 69
© Joseph Sohm; ChromoSohm Inc./CORBIS, 15
©David and Peter Turnley/CORBIS, 40
© Pablo Coral Vega/CORBIS, 47
© David H. Wells/CORBIS, 78

About the Author

Peggy J. Parks holds a bachelor of science degree from Aquinas College in Grand Rapids, Michigan, where she graduated magna cum laude. She worked in the marketing and advertising field for ten years before becoming a full-time freelance writer in 1995. Parks was the profile writer for *Grand Rapids: The City That Works*, a book that is part of Towery Publications' Urban Tapestries series. She has written newspaper and magazine articles as well as corporate publications, executive speeches, public relations campaigns, and websites for a variety of clients. Parks lives in Muskegon, Michigan, a town she says inspires her writing because of its location on the shores of Lake Michigan.